Wilhelm Ihne

Early Rome from the Foundation of the City to its Destruction

Fifth Edition

Wilhelm Ihne

Early Rome from the Foundation of the City to its Destruction
Fifth Edition

ISBN/EAN: 9783337379834

Printed in Europe, USA, Canada, Australia, Japan

Cover: Foto ©ninafisch / pixelio.de

More available books at **www.hansebooks.com**

EPOCHS OF ANCIENT HISTORY

EARLY ROME

FROM THE FOUNDATION OF THE CITY TO ITS DESTRUCTION BY THE GAULS

BY

W. IHNE, Ph.D.

PROFESSOR AT THE UNIVERSITY OF HEIDELBERG
AUTHOR OF 'THE HISTORY OF ROME'

WITH A MAP

FIFTH EDITION

LONDON
LONGMANS, GREEN, AND CO.
AND NEW YORK: 15 EAST 16th STREET
1888

WHO list the Roman greatness forth to figure,
Him needeth not to seek for usage right
Of line, or lead, or rule, or square to measure
Her length, her breadth, her deepness and her hight;
But him behoves to view in compass round
All that the Ocean grasps in his long arms,
Be it where th' yearly star doth scorch the ground,
Or where cold Boreas blows his bitter storms.
Rome was th' whole world and all the world was Rome;
And if things named their names do equalize,
When land and sea you name, **then name ye Rome.**
And naming Rome ye land and sea comprize !
For th' ancient plot of Rome displayed **plain**
The map of all the wide world doth contain.

All that which Egypt whilom did devise,
All that which Greece their temples to embrave
After th' Ionick, **Attick,** Dorick guise,
Or Corinth, skilled in curious work to grave;
All that Lysippus' **practick art** could form,
Apelles' wit, **or Phidias his skill,**
Was wont this ancient **city to adorn,**
And heaven itself with her **wide wonders fill :**
All that which Athens ever brought forth wise
Or that which Africk ever brought **forth strange,**
All that which Asia ever had of prise,
Was here to see. O marvellous great change !
Rome living was the world's **sole ornament,**
And dead, is now the **world's sole moniment !**

      Spenser, *Ruins of Rome.*

PREFACE.

HISTORICAL criticism has now for more than half a century been actively at work upon the history of Rome, and the tests which, in accordance with the laws of evidence, it has applied to the traditional narrative, have shown that the greater part of the tales which have passed for more than two thousand years as the history of the Roman kings and of the earlier ages of the republic, contain but a small portion of truth hidden under a huge mass of fiction. The results of scientific investigation have gradually been accepted by all scholars whose judgment is not perverted by an obstinate historical conservatism very much akin to superstition; and the present volume is an attempt to give these results in a form intelligible to any reader of common capacity, and possessed of so much previous knowledge as can be acquired, or ought to be acquired, at an average school before the age of fifteen or sixteen. All purely scientific matter has been excluded. The results have been given with only so much of argument and proof as is absolutely necessary to carry conviction. All scientific references and notes have been excluded. Yet no statement has been made which could not be substantiated by reference to the original authors from whom all our information is derived. It is hoped that those readers who are attracted by the subject, and wish to carry their studies further, will be able to use the present volume as a starting point for investigations of their own.

W. IHNE.

FELSECK, HEIDELBERG:
September 12. 1875.

CONTENTS.

CHAPTER I.
THE CAUSES OF THE GREATNESS OF ROME.

	PAGE
The greatness of the Roman empire	1
Its influence on modern civilisation	1
The Roman law	2
Political wisdom of the Roman people	2
Value of the history of Rome	3
The small beginning of Rome	3
The advantage of Rome over other Italian cities	4
Geographical situation	4
Race	4
Men of genius	5
The site of Rome	6
Proximity of the seven hills to each other	6
Political association	7
Secondary causes	8

CHAPTER II.
SOURCES OF THE HISTORY OF ROME.

The meaning of history	9
Character of early history	10
The credulity of the old historians	10
Origin of historical criticism	11
Niebuhr	11
Niebuhr's influence	12
Sir G. C. Lewis	12
Line of demarcation between fable and history	12
Tests of historical truth	13
Contemporary evidence	13
Second-hand evidence	13
Tradition	14
The oldest Roman annalists	14

Contents.

	PAGE
Fabius Pictor	14
Cincius Alimentus	14
Porcius Cato	14
Later annalists	15
Historical poems	16
Sources of the annalists	16
Scarcity of fiction pure and simple	17
Existence of a traditional story before Fabius	17
Non-existence of a national epos	18
Oral tradition	18
Importance of the knowledge of precedents and customary laws	18
The senate as conservator of the memory of the past	19
The sacerdotal corporations	19
Probability of a pontifical narrative	20
Oral tradition alone insufficient to account for the detail of the annals	20
The pontifical or great annals	21
Age of the pontifical annals	22
Other public documents	22
Laws and treaties	23
Laws of the twelve tables	23
Apocryphal laws of the kings	23
Legendary relics	23
Public monuments	24
Fixity and continuity of the Roman families	24
Their aristocratic spirit and pride	25
Family portraits	26
Solemn funerals	26
Funeral orations	26
Written laudations	26
Family chronicles	27
Their antiquity	27
And character	27
General character of the earliest annals	28
Family traditions confined to the republican period	29
Different treatment of the regal and the republican period in the annals	29
Reasons for noticing the legends of the kings	30

CHAPTER III.

THE LEGENDS OF THE SEVEN KINGS OF ROME.

	PAGE
The legend of Aeneas the Trojan	30
Birth of Romulus and Remus	31
Dispute between Romulus and Remus	32
Building of Rome by Romulus	32
Death of Remus	32
The asylum of Romulus	33
Rape of the Sabines	33
Tarpeia	33
War of the Romans and Sabines	34
Mettius Curtius	34
Union of the Romans and the Sabines	35
The laws of Romulus	35
Death of Romulus	36
The first interregnum	37
Numa Pompilius, the second king	37
His sacred laws	37
His civil laws	39
The peace of Numa	39
Tullus Hostilius, the third king	40
War with Alba	40
The Horatii and Curiatii	41
Crime of Horatius	42
Treason of Mettius	42
Destruction of Alba	43
Tullus's wickedness and death	43
Ancus Marcius, the fourth king	43
War with the Latins	44
Lucumo of Tarquinii	44
Lucius Tarquinius, the fifth king	45
Wars with the Latins and Sabines	45
The reforms of Tarquinius	46
Temple of Jupiter on the Capitol	47
The great sewer, forum, and circus	47
Miraculous birth of Servius Tullius	47
Servius Tullius, the sixth king	49
The centuriate assembly of the people	50
Murder of King Servius	52

	PAGE
Lucius Tarquinius, the seventh king	53
Conquest of Gabii	54
Establishment of Roman power over Latium	54
Purchase of the Sibylline books	55
Message to Delphi	55
Outrage of Sextus on Lucretia	56
Expulsion of the king and establishment of the republic	57
Conspiracy for the restoration of the king	58
The patriotism of Brutus	58
Banishment of the house of the Tarquinii	59
War with Tarquinii and Veii	59
War with Porsenna of Clusium	60
Horatius Cocles	60
Mucius Scaevola	61
Cloelia	62
The Etruscans defeated at Aricia	62
Latin war	62
Battle of Lake Regillus	63

CHAPTER IV.

EXAMINATION OF THE LEGENDS OF THE KINGS.

Absence of contemporary records	63
Rationalist explanation of fables	64
Moral impossibilities	65
Chronological impossibilities	65
Other objections	67
Omnipotent lawgivers	67
Laws and religion as primeval as language	68
Aetiological myths	69
The rape of the Sabines	69
The Lacus Curtius	70
Greek stories	71
The legend of Romulus not of Roman origin	72
Meagreness of Roman imagination	73
Repetitions	73
Identity of Romulus and Tullus	74
Of Numa and Ancus	74
Of the two Tarquins, Romulus and Tullus	75
Servius Tullius	75

Contents.

	PAGE
The latter part of the history of the kings as fabulous as the first	75
The miraculous origin of the Servian constitution	76
Expulsion of Tarquinius equally miraculous	77
Incredibility of the foreign history	78
The war of Porsenna resulted in the subjugation of Rome	78
The Latin war full of fictions	80

CHAPTER V.
THE FIVE PHASES OF THE HISTORY OF ROME IN THE REGAL PERIOD.

Most ancient state of Latium	81
A confederacy under Alba as head	82
Rome a Latin settlement	82
Invasion of Latium by Sabines	82
Alliance of Romans and Sabines	83
Alliance developed into a federal state	84
The sacerdotal king superseded by a military king	85
The Etruscans	85
Etruscan dominion in Latium	85
Reforms of Tarquin and Servius	86
Effect of the military monarchy	87
The revolution	87
The republic	87

CHAPTER VI.
RELIGIOUS INSTITUTIONS IN THE TIME OF THE KINGS.

Materials for a sketch	88
The epic poetry of Greece	89
Conservative spirit of the Romans	90
Great antiquity of religious institutions	90
Supremacy of religion in the East	90
Every religion purely national	91
Hierarchical character of civil communities	91
Political institutions originally religious	91
The religion of the Romans	92
Adoption of the Greek mythology	93
Minute religious observances	94

	PAGE
Meaning of the word 'religion'	95
Religion as a legal system	95
Pontiffs and other priests	96
Various forms of divination	97
The auspices	98
Abuse of the auspices	99
Genuine faith of the old time	99

CHAPTER VII.
CHARACTER OF THE MONARCHY.

The king was high priest	100
Inauguration of the king	100
Mode of election	101
Criminal judges appointed by the king	101
Military commanders	101
Sacerdotal kings superseded by military chiefs	102
Pontiffs appointed after the abolition of the sacerdotal royalty	103

CHAPTER VIII.
THE SENATE OF THE REGAL PERIOD.

The fathers *de facto* representatives of the great houses	104
The authority of the fathers	105
The interregnum	106
Conflict between the senate and the later kings	106

CHAPTER IX.
THE PEOPLE IN THE REGAL PERIOD.

The people. Patricians and plebeians	107
Patrician assembly of curiae	108
The three different popular assemblies	109
Rights of the plebeians	110
Origin of the plebs	110
The clients	111
The military kings the patrons of the plebs	111

CHAPTER X.
THE MAGISTRATES OF THE REPUBLIC.

Change in the executive	112
The consular office	113
Limited in time	113

Contents.

Its partition among two colleagues	113
Right of intercession	113
The dictatorship	114
Origin of the dictatorship	115
Valerius Poplicola	115
The Valerian laws	116
Duties of the consular office	117
Administration of justice	117
Private jurisdiction	117
The priests public servants	118
The pontiffs the interpreters of divine and human law	118
And the guardians of science and learning	119
The augurs	120

CHAPTER XI.
THE SENATE OF THE REPUBLIC.

The senate a consultative body	122
Number of senators	122
New senators added after the expulsion of Tarquin were not plebeians	122
Nor were the new members plebeians raised to the rank of patricians	124
The senate purely patrician and champion of patrician interests	124
The title *patres conscripti*	124
Difference of the senate from modern parliaments	125
The senate not a representative assembly	125
Mode of electing senators	126
Character and stability of the senate	126

CHAPTER XII.
THE POPULAR ASSEMBLIES OF THE REPUBLIC.

The proper functions of the popular assemblies	127
The comitia curiata superseded	127
The comitia centuriata	128
Military character of the comitia centuriata	128
Functions of the comitia	129
Alleged origin of the comitia curiata	129

xvi   *Contents.*

	PAGE
Forms observed at the meetings of the comitia centuriata	131
Prevalence of patrician power in the state	131
Probable origin of the comitia centuriata	133
The assembly of centuries ceases to be military and becomes purely political	134

CHAPTER XIII.
THE TRIBUNES OF THE PEOPLE.

Secession of the plebs	135
The causes of the secession	136
Original power of the tribune	137
Plebeian aediles	137
The sacred law	137
Antiquity of the tribuneship	138
Control of the conscription by the tribunes	138
Number of tribunes	139
Original mode of election	139
The comitia curiata	139
Division of the land into local tribes	140
Plebeian character of the comitia tributa	141
The comitia tributa recognized as a sovereign assembly	141
Number of local tribes	142

CHAPTER XIV.
THE AGRARIAN LAW OF SPURIUS CASSIUS.

Wealth and poverty	143
Disposal of conquered land	143
Rise of discontent among the plebeians	144
The agrarian laws	144
The proposals of Spurius Cassius	144

CHAPTER XV.
THE LEAGUE WITH THE LATINS AND HERNICANS.

Prevalence of confederations	145
Rome the head of a pre-historic league	146
New league between Rome and Latium	146
Motives for concluding the league	147
Object and effect of the league	147

CHAPTER XVI.

THE WARS WITH THE VOLSCIANS AND AEQUIANS.

	PAGE
The story of Coriolanus	149
Criticism of the story of Coriolanus	151
Effect of the Volscian wars	153
The story of Cincinnatus	153
Exaggerations of the story	155
Character of the Aequian wars	155

CHAPTER XVII.

WAR WITH THE ETRUSCANS.

The Etruscan town of Fidenae	156
Roman fort on the Cremera	156
Story of the Fabii	157
Historical foundation of the story	158

CHAPTER XVIII.

THE DECEMVIRS AND THE LAWS OF THE TWELVE TABLES.
451–442 B.C.

The Publilian law	159
Advancing claims of the plebeians	160
The Terentilian rogations	160
The Claudian family	161
Concessions to the plebs	162
Election of decemvirs	162
The laws of the Twelve Tables	162
Perplexities of the annalistic accounts	163
Embassy to Athens	163
Reasons for rejecting the story	164
The traditional story of the decemvirs	165
Criticism of the story	167
The laws of the last two tables	168
Probable causes of the overthrow of the decemvirs	168

CHAPTER XIX.

EXTENSION OF PLEBEIAN RIGHTS FROM 449 TO 390 B.C.

	PAGE
Bearing of the decemviral legislation on public and private laws	169
Quaestors elected by the people	169
Right of appeal confirmed and extended	170
Restoration of the tribuneship and aedileship	170
Sovereignty of the assembly of tribes acknowledged	170
Extension of the legislative and elective functions of the assembly of tribes	171
Gradual abolition of patrician privileges	171
Canuleian law on the intermarriage of patricians and plebeians	171
Agitation for a share in the executive	172
The office of military tribunes with consular power	172
Policy of the patricians to make the laws nugatory	173
Explanation of this result	174
Spurius Maelius	175
The censorship	176
Duration of the office of censors	177
Extent of the power of the censors in drawing up the list of citizens	178
Nomination of senators	179
Revision of the centuries of knights	180
The censorship of morals	180
Financial duties of the censors	181
Limitation of the censorship to eighteen months	181
Doubling of the number of quaestors	181
Plebeians elected to the office of military tribunes	182

CHAPTER XX.

THE FOREIGN RELATIONS OF ROME DOWN TO THE CONQUEST OF VEII.

The position of Rome in Latium	182
Condition of Latium	183
Decay of the Volscians and Aequians	183
Increased preponderance of Rome	184
Acquisition of the territory of Corioli	184
Conquest of Labici, Bolae, and other towns in Latium	185
Conquest of Fidenae	185
The *spolia opima* of Cornelius Cossus	185

Contents.

	PAGE
The city of Veii	186
Hostilities between Veii and Rome	187
New military organization of Camillus	188
The Roman armies	188
Introduction of military pay	189
Siege of Veii	190
Miraculous capture of Veii	190
Criticism of the story	191

CHAPTER XXI.

THE INVASION OF THE GAULS.

Decline of Etruscan power	194
Migration of the Gauls	194
Their invasion of Etruria	195
Cause of war with Rome	195
Battle of the Allia	196
Rome abandoned	197
Defence of the Capitol	198
Camillus appointed dictator	198
The Capitol saved by M. Manlius	199
Ransom paid to the Gauls	199
Expulsion of the Gauls	200
Criticism of the story	200
The destruction of Rome less complete than reported	200
Long duration of the blockade improbable	201
The story of Camillus	202
Contradicted by Polybius	202
The story of the geese an aetiological legend	203
Index	205

MAP.

Ancient Latium and adjoining districts . . *Frontispiece*

EARLY ROME.

CHAPTER I.

THE CAUSES OF THE GREATNESS OF ROME.

THE Roman Empire in the early ages of our era embraced all the countries round the Mediterranean Sea, together with vast tracts north of the Alps, stretching in one direction as far as the Danube, and even beyond that river in its lower course, and in another as far as the Atlantic Ocean, St George's Channel, the Solway Frith, and the North Sea. In this great empire was gathered up the sum total that remained of the religions, laws, customs, languages, letters, arts, and sciences of all the nations of antiquity which had successively held sway or predominance. It was the appointed task of the Romans to collect the product of all this mass of varied national labour as a common treasure of mankind, and to deliver it over to the ages which were to follow. *The greatness of the Roman Empire.*

When after the lapse of centuries Europe gradually emerged from the flood of barbarism which had overwhelmed it, and new nations were formed out of the wreck of the Roman Empire, it was the treasure of ancient learning saved by Rome which guided the first steps of these nations towards new forms of civilised life. The language and literature of Rome had never been altogether lost and forgotten. *Its influence on modern civilisation.*

By slow degrees the tongue of Latium was moulded into the dialects of Italy, Spain, Portugal, and France. The Christian Church pertinaciously clung to the old language which was that of her ritual and of the Latin Fathers. The city of Rome had become the seat of the successors of St. Peter, and her language penetrated wherever Roman Catholic missionaries preached the Gospel of Christ. It became the vehicle of all the learning of the time, the language of diplomacy, of law and government; finally, of education; and in the schools and universities of modern Europe the whole world of Latin literature was fostered into a second life, and acquired an influence on the public mind of which every living man still in some way or other feels the effects. But the Latin literature, though great and admirable in many respects, is not the grandest product of the Roman mind. It was not original or spontaneous, and consequently not truly national. In poetry, philosophy, and history the Romans were the disciples and imitators of the Greeks. They added little of their own. Their strength and originality lay in another direction. They proved themselves masters in the art of civil law and government. The Roman law possesses an intrinsic excellence which has made it the foundation of all legal study in Europe, and the model of almost all codes of civil law now in force. Every one of us is benefited directly or indirectly by this legacy of the Roman people, a legacy as valuable as the literary and artistic models which we owe to the great writers and sculptors of Greece.

The Roman law.

The stupendous growth of the Roman Empire, and the solidity of its structure, which enabled it to last so long, are due not so much to the courage and endurance of the Roman soldiers, nor to the genius of the Roman generals, as to other

Political wisdom of the Roman people.

causes, and chiefly to the combination of a desire for improvement with a respect for established rights: in short, to political wisdom, which prefers reform to revolution, which is not dazzled by speculation on impossible perfection, and which never sacrifices what is good in order to attain what may appear to be best. The development of the Roman constitution differs in this respect from the usual course of Greek policy, and reminds us of the spirit in which the English constitution was built up, in which whatever is new is an outgrowth and development of something old, and in which mere speculation and theoretic enthusiasm have never been able to sever the link which connects the present with the past.

The history of the Roman people, then, has surely many claims on our attention. It is to a certain extent the history of every modern nation in its earlier stages, and it contains lessons of policy, which even after so many centuries are instructive and may prove applicable in the political conflicts of the present day. *Value of the history of Rome.*

No great state known to history can be traced to such a small beginning as Rome. When the kings of Persia and of Macedon built up their respective monarchies, they worked with the national power which they found ready for them, waiting only to be organized and directed. The Carthaginians started on their career of enterprise and conquest with the experience, the skill, and the wealth of their Phœnician mother country. The Romans, on the other hand, when they emerged to power in Latium and Etruria, could boast neither of a numerous nor a civilised ancestry; they had found no accumulation of wealth ready for their use, no political experience which they might have applied. They had everything to make from the beginning; they *The small beginning of Rome.*

had to form a nation and a national character, to create national wealth, to acquire political experience. They succeeded in all this, and so vigorous was the spirit which animated the citizens of that single city, that it infused itself into the population of all Italy, and to a certain extent of the ancient world, and thus the language, customs, thought, and religion of numerous nations were Romanised, and exhibit traces of their origin even at the present day.

What was the cause, we may well ask, that gave such a superiority to Rome over other cities of Italy? Why did not Veii, or Naples, or Syracuse become the nucleus of a great empire? Had Rome an advantage over them with regard to soil, climate, or geographical situation? This question must be answered in the negative. The soil in the neighbourhood of Rome was comparatively sterile, the climate unhealthy, the situation unfavourable for commerce. The city had no good port, nor was there a large fertile country behind it which might have supplied materials for export and markets for foreign goods.

The advantage of Rome over other Italian cities

Geographical situation

If Rome had no such advantages, was it to any advantages of race and descent that she owed her eminence? Again we must answer in the negative. The people of Rome were of the same race as their neighbours. They could boast of no superiority on the score of descent. For a long time indeed the fable of the descent from Aeneas and his Trojan followers had currency. This fable is now exploded, and if it were not, we should hardly infer that for their political and military greatness the Romans were indebted to Oriental ancestors. More recently an admixture of Etruscans has been inferred from indications more or less significant. But this admixture has not as yet been

Race.

proved by any satisfactory evidence, and moreover the political and religious systems, as well as the language of the Etruscans, were entirely different from those of the Latin or other neighbouring tribes. The Sabines and Latins, who combined to form the fundamental element of the Roman people, were offshoots of the Sabellian stock to which all the native or aboriginal population of Italy belong, from the Apennines south of the Po to the extreme end of the peninsula.

It was therefore not superiority of race which gave the Romans predominance in Italy. We must look for another cause. Perhaps we may be led to surmise that it was a fortunate succession of great men which raised the Romans above the other Italian communities. We know that the Persian, the Macedonian, the Arab empires owed their rapid rise to the genius of individuals. In modern Europe the aggrandisement of Prussia is due in some considerable degree to the eminent political and military qualities of the Hohenzollern dynasty. But Rome was singularly sterile in great men. She was made powerful and predominant by the almost unheeded labour of a vast number of citizens of average ability, not by men whose names have the ring of Solon, Pericles, Epaminondas, or Alexander; or, if we compare modern times, of Charlemagne, Peter the Great, Frederic, or Washington. The kings and statesmen to whom the establishment of the State and the laws is ascribed, such as Romulus, Numa, Servius, and Brutus, belong not to authentic history, but to prehistoric fable; and when politicians arose who exerted an influence beyond that of private citizens in the service of the State, men who, like Sulla and Cæsar, wielded in their hands the power of the whole community, the greatness of republican Rome had passed away.

Men of genius.

If then the first cause of Roman greatness, the first

impulse given to national development, is to be found neither in the advantages of soil and situation, nor in the superiority of race, nor in the genius of great men, shall we be driven to say that it was mere chance, or, in more reverent language, Divine providence which selected Rome as the seat of empire over Italy and the world? Such a conclusion would not be a solution of the problem, but an evasion of the difficulty and a confession of weakness unworthy of the spirit of historical enquiry. Providence does not act contrary but according to fixed laws, and it is for us to investigate these laws, not to ignore them. Nor is it utterly impossible to discover the cause to which Rome owed in her infancy such an accession of strength as secured to her the superiority over her neighbours, and thus laid the foundation of her future greatness.

If we compare the site of Rome with the sites of the numerous cities which simultaneously with the earliest settlements on the seven hills covered the plain of Latium and the adjoining hills, we find that each of the other towns was built on some steep or easily defended hill. Some of these hill-towns, such as Praeneste, were actually stronger than either the Roman Capitol or the Palatine hill. But nowhere do we find, as on the Tiber, a group *of hills* possessing each the advantage of defensibility, and yet lying so close to one another that the political isolation of each was impossible and that some kind of combination or federation for the maintenance of internal peace became absolutely necessary. People who live at a distance from each other may indulge in occasional strife; but if by proximity of habitation they are compelled to have daily intercourse with one another, they are obliged to agree upon some terms of amicable life, if they do not prefer the miseries which internecine war must entail on all. This

The site of Rome.

Proximity of the seven hills to each other.

was the condition of the various settlements on the seven hills, which lay so near together that nature itself seemed to have destined them to form a combined city. There are dim, half fabulous traditions which speak of wars waged between the people of the Quirinal hill and that of the Palatine. But the same traditions also report an amicable settlement of the combats, an agreement to live in peace, a combined government of the respective chiefs; in fact, they describe a confederation of the two peoples, and their combination into one political community. Nor are these facts traceable only in the traditions of the Roman people; they are equally so in their institutions. The association of the Roman *gentes* (houses) to form *curiae* (wards), and of these to form the three tribes of Ramnes, Tities, and Luceres, together with other indications of a gradual union of independent bodies to form the Roman people, show clearly enough that the principle of association lay at the root of the early vigour of Rome, and gave to the combined people of the Romans and the Sabines (*populus Romanus Quiritium*) such a preponderance over each isolated Latin city, that Rome alone became fit to be the head of Latium.

Thus then arose a spirit of political association based upon calculations of interest but sanctioned by the sense of right; nor when it had accomplished its first task, the security of the seven hills, did it die away, but continued to work on a larger scale when Rome had become great. City after city and tribe after tribe were invited or compelled to join the leading power as allies (*socii*) until the whole of Italy, though in fact subject to Rome, appeared to be only one vast confederacy.

<small>Political association.</small>

We have seen that the geographical position of Rome, and the peculiarity of race, cannot be deemed to have been the first causes of Roman greatness. Now, however, after we have discovered the first cause, we may and must admit that both these circumstances power- fully contributed as secondary causes to ac- celerate and consolidate the growth of Rome, when it had taken root owing to the peculiar formation of the ground. The comparative sterility of the territory encouraged the warlike spirit of the early Romans, whose frequent wars seem to have been undertaken oftener for the sake of booty than in just self-defence. It is possible too, that the unhealthiness of the surrounding district at certain seasons of the year may have served as a barrier to ward off attacks, when other resources failed. The remoteness of the sea and the want of a good port was a protection from the numerous pirates who infested the Tyrrhenian waters. But it was especially the situation of Rome in the middle of the peninsula, cutting off the northern from the southern half, which enabled her to divide her enemies and to subdue them separately. Lastly, the similarity of race, which bound the Romans by the ties of blood and common customs to the Latins and the Samnites, the Campanians, Lucanians, and in fact to all the indigenous races of Italy, enabled them to repel the invasions of their non-Italian enemies, the Gauls and the Carthaginians, and to appear in the light of champions and protectors of Italy. When in the time of the first historical inroad of the Gauls the onset of these barbarians had been broken by the brave defenders of the Capitol, Rome rose from her ashes as by a second birth with the title to pre-eminence among all the peoples of Italy; and when the proud and able Hannibal was foiled before the same walls, Rome in a still more signal and decisive manner fought at the head of the Italians against the common foe.

<small>Secondary causes.</small>

CHAPTER II.

SOURCES OF THE HISTORY OF ROME.

WE purpose, in the present volume, to trace the history of Rome through its earliest stages, from the foundation of the city to its destruction by the Gauls, or, in the language of the old annalists, from Romulus, its first founder, to its second founder, Camillus. We shall have to review a period of nominally three centuries and a half, a period as long as that which separates us from the Protestant Reformation, from Luther and Charles V. and Henry VIII. It is the period in which those institutions were formed which proved the strength of the strongest republic of all ages. It is, therefore, a period replete with interest for those students of history who desire to penetrate, as it were, into the workshop of the national mind, and to watch its operations. And yet we can hardly speak of a history of this time, except in so far as we attach to the word 'history' the original meaning which it bore in the Greek language, and which is synonymous with 'investigation.' History, in its modern sense, not only endeavours to ascertain events accurately, but also to show how each successive event was the product of what preceded and the cause of what followed. Such a concatenation of cause and effect is possible only where the facts can be ascertained not only with certainty, but also with circumstantiality. Where these conditions do not exist, inquiry may still be carried on with profit and with pleasure; truth may be elicited and errors laid bare; but the full delight and the satisfaction produced by genuine history are wanting.

The meaning of 'history.'

The introductory chapters in the history of every

country necessarily consist of such investigations. They are the dawn preceding the day; they contain truth mixed with fables in ever-varying proportions; they are often more perplexing and irritating than instructive and pleasing, and yet we must make our way through them, for as every succeeding event can only be understood if we know that which preceded and prepared it, we are impelled to ascend the stream of history as high as we can, even if the source itself should be hidden and inaccessible.

<small>Character of early history.</small>

The ancient historians, and the modern ones too, until quite recently, were not disturbed by any doubts concerning the truth of the early chapters of the history of Rome. They related, with implicit and childlike faith, the foundation of the city, which took place, they say, on the 21st of April in a year calculated as identical with the second year of the seventh Olympiad, or 754 years before the Christian era. They related the wars of Romulus, the legislation of Numa, the conquests of Tullus, and, in short, the deeds of all the kings with the same air of faith with which they described events reported by eye-witnesses. It is true they were occasionally puzzled by contradictions in the narrative, or startled by some downright incredible statement; they were consequently forced to abandon as mere ornaments the reported miracles, but they never doubted that what remained of this narrative was substantially true. This simple faith was the delight of Cicero and Livy, of Dionysius and Plutarch, and of all the following ages down almost to our own. Neither the cautious and sober-minded Bacon nor the learned Milton doubted the truth of a story hallowed by the implicit faith of so many ages. And yet the revival of learning in the fifteenth century had hardly taken place before some

<small>The credulity of the old historians.</small>

acute and bold enquirers began in a modest and tentative way to point out errors and improbabilities in some of the received accounts. Yet a few isolated glimpses of light left the general darkness unbroken. *Origin of historical criticism.* Even the more comprehensive view of the unhistoric character of the early history of Rome, which was taken by the Italian philosopher G. Vico (d. 1744) produced no effect upon the general convictions of historians. Vico's remarks were still unheeded when two Frenchmen — Pouilly in 1729, and Beaufort in 1738 — published treatises on the uncertainty of the first five centuries of Roman history, in which, for the first time, a series of doubts was not only expressed, but supported by sound arguments. Yet even Pouilly and Beaufort seemed to have found no followers. Neither the philosophic jurist Montesquieu (d. 1755), nor the sceptic historians Hume (d. 1776) and Gibbon (d. 1794), seem to have been shaken in their faith. At last, in 1811, B. G. Niebuhr published the first volume of a learned and searching criticism into the *Niebuhr.* history of Rome, in which he showed how utterly untenable the stories are which had so long passed unchallenged as the history of the Roman kings and of the first ages of the republic. Niebuhr's book was written at the right time. The minds of the literary world were prepared to receive the truth, and from that moment to the present the critical, that is, the rational, study of Roman history has gained ground more and more; every year has added contributions to our knowledge of Roman institutions, laws, government, antiquities, and the languages of ancient Italy. The same method of critical investigation has since been applied to the histories of Greece and other nations; and though Niebuhr's views have, in many respects, been modified and rejected, the ante-Niebuhrian mode of treating history, and especially the history of Rome, has been abandoned by the unanimous consent of modern historians.

When Niebuhr's book first appeared, it caused amazement and not a little regret, that such a number of stories, *Niebuhr's influence.* endeared like household words to our earliest recollections, should be rejected as useless and idle fancies. This feeling, however, which in sterner minds assumed even the character of indignation and stubborn conservatism, has almost subsided. The critical method has so far gained ground that, on the whole, Niebuhr is more blamed for retaining so much of the old faith than for overturning so many vain idols. The most *Sir G. C. Lewis.* advanced in this line of criticism is Sir George Cornewall Lewis, who, in his able and comprehensive book 'on the Credibility of Early Roman History,' published in 1855, discussed the question in all its bearings, and came to the conclusion that a genuine and trustworthy history of Rome does not begin before the war with Pyrrhus; that is to say, the second half of the fifth century after the foundation of the city.

In this conclusion Sir G. C. Lewis seems to have gone too far. It is, of course, difficult to draw the exact line *Line of demarcation between fable and history.* which divides darkness from light and error from truth, when one passes into the other by imperceptible gradations. Wherever we may draw the line, some truth will always be found to be mixed up with error, and some error to contain particles of truth; and in proportion as men are severe or lax in their canons of criticism, they will be inclined to limit or to extend the legitimate domain of history. After all, sufficient data remain for sketching the outline of historical events from the beginning of the republic, and to form a conception of the condition of the Roman people even in the age of the kings.

The first question we have to answer, if we would

judge of the credibility of a statement claiming to be considered historical, is not whether it is probable or likely; for the fictions of a novel or a poem may be extremely likely without having the least pretence to veracity. We must ask, What is the evidence upon which the statement rests? Were the witnesses able and were they willing to tell the truth? All historical narratives must be derived from contemporary evidence, from persons who have heard or seen what they report, and who do not purposely corrupt, distort, or altogether falsify the facts. Inaccuracy, incompleteness, faulty apprehension, we must expect and excuse even in the best of witnesses, for experience shows that facts, as they pass through the observing and reasoning mind of witnesses, inevitably assume that particular form and colour which the individuality of these witnesses gives to them. We may even expect contradictions as to detail, degree, and manner. In partial and passionate witnesses we may look for involuntary or even voluntary misrepresentations. All such divergencies in the statements of eye-witnesses it is the duty of the historian to weigh against each other, and from their combination to work out the truth. *Tests of historical truth. Contemporary evidence*

This task becomes more difficult and the result more precarious, if we obtain our evidence not from eye-witnesses, but at second-hand from persons who report not what they have seen and heard, but what has been related to them by others. All the causes which tend to distort truth are now doubled, or more than doubled. To the errors, wilful or involuntary, of the original witnesses are added those of the secondary witnesses, and the errors increase in number and magnitude the further our witnesses are removed in time and place from the original actors of the events which they relate. It is, indeed, possible that *Second-hand evidence.*

even when accounts have been thus transmitted through a line of successive reporters, they may still in the main bear some resemblance—nay, that they may give the substance or the main features of the original facts. In such a case we have before us a *genuine tradition*, which is available for many purposes of historical study, and which constitutes the chief portion of all true historical knowledge possessed by any people before history begins to be cultivated as a branch of literature. But it is evident that very little trust can be placed in the detail of such traditions, and that perfect accuracy even in the essential parts can hardly be expected.

<small>Tradition.</small>

Let us now see what degree of confidence the history of the regal period of Rome may claim on the score of external evidence.

More than five hundred years had passed since the alleged foundation of Rome in 754, before the first rude and feeble attempts were made by a Roman to write a continuous history of the people from the earliest ages. Fabius Pictor, a member of one of the noblest families, himself actively engaged in the military and civil service of the State, during the war with Hannibal, wrote a history of his time, and prefixed to it by way of introduction a short narrative of the whole preceding period. A similar work was undertaken by Lucius Cincius Alimentus, a contemporary of Fabius Pictor. Both these authors wrote not in Latin, but in Greek, evidently because the Latin language in their time seemed not sufficiently cultivated for literary composition, and because they had before their eyes as models the great historians of Greece. The first who applied the Latin language to historical composition was Marcus Porcius Cato, the famous censor, who as a young man had served in the war with Hannibal, and

<small>The oldest Roman annalists.</small>

<small>Fabius Pictor.</small>

<small>Cincius Alimentus.</small>

<small>Porcius Cato.</small>

died shortly before the final destruction of Carthage (149 B.C.), of which he was one of the chief instigators. Cato may be looked upon as the originator of Latin prose writing for literary purposes, and it is curious and instructive to notice that the Romans occupied this field nearly 300 years later than the Greeks. Cato wrote the history of his time, giving a prominent place in it to his own exploits, and even to his own speeches, and he, like his predecessors, prefixed several chapters on the history of the earlier ages, including therein accounts of the origin of other Italian cities besides Rome, whence the title of the book, 'Origines,' was derived.

From this time forward we find a considerable number of Roman writers engaged in the same task. The most prominent among them were Lucius Cassius Hemina, Lucius Calpurnius Piso, Valerius Antias, Quintus Claudius Quadrigarius, and Caius Licinius Macer, reaching from the time of the Punic wars to the age of Sulla. *Later annalists.* Their writings, like those of their predecessors, are lost ; but it appears from some notices in extant writers, and from a few remaining fragments, that the object of these men was more to compose striking and entertaining narratives, and to flatter the national pride of their countrymen, than to give plain and faithful accounts of the events. They endeavoured to distinguish themselves as writers of the Latin tongue, and to rival their Greek models. In this endeavour, it must be admitted, they signally failed. Though they preferred not only rhetorical flourishes to simple style, but also fictitious and ornamental detail to truth gained by patient research, they are looked down upon by Cicero and Tacitus as meagre and frigid chroniclers. As their works followed one another, they grew in bulk and pretensions, but not in trustworthiness. Some of them, in the time of civil commotions, were influenced even by party spirit. This class of writers, designated by the common name of 'annalists,' supplied the extant historians, especially Livy and Dionysius, with the materials for their works. And it appears that unfortunately Livy followed chiefly the fuller and more elaborate, but less truthful accounts of the younger annalists, especially those of Valerius Antias, the least conscientious of them all.

Whilst the annalists set themselves the task of simply recording the history of their own or preceding times, we find that contemporaneously with Fabius and Cincius, two poets, Naevius and Ennius, moulded the same materials into epic poems. Naevius (d. 204 B.C.) wrote the history of the first Punic war in the old Saturnian verse, the national metre of the Romans, which was soon superseded by the hexameter, imported from Greece. Ennius, a younger contemporary of Naevius (d. 169 B.C.) composed a poem in hexameters on the second Punic war. Both poets prefixed to the account of their own time the legendary and traditional history of early times from Aeneas downwards. Of these poems a few scanty fragments are preserved, from which we can gather that their authors adopted in the main the current notions of the early history of Rome, and that they adorned the facts according to the exigencies of their poetical aims. But it seems unlikely that they had access to any other sources of information than the annalists, and therefore their works could not have been more authentic and trustworthy as sources of the history of Rome: nor does it appear that any either of the annalists or the extant historians looked upon them or cited them as historical witnesses.

Historical poems.

In so far as the annalists and annalistic poets related the events which happened in their own time or in the age immediately before their own, they may have been trustworthy witnesses; but we may

Sources of the annalists

ask what they could possibly know of events preceding their birth by centuries. What, for instance, were the sources from which Fabius Pictor, in the second century before Christ, derived the details of the war with Pyrrhus in the third, or of the wars with the Samnites in the fourth, of the Volscian and Aequian wars in the fifth, and the whole chronicle of the kings in the sixth, seventh, and even eighth centuries before the Christian era?

Of one thing we may be quite certain; the annalists did not simply invent the substance of their narrative, certainly not the whole of it. The task would have been too much for the dry, frigid, and unproductive imagination of a Roman. If, on the other hand, a Greek had concocted the account, it would have been far more lively than it is, more interesting, and full of startling occurrences, and would shine in all the varied hues of the exuberant fancy with which that brilliant race was endowed. The stories were evidently not invented by Romans, nor could they, such as we know them, have been invented by Greeks. Besides which, on the whole, the divergencies and contradictions which they contain affect only the detail of the narrative. A uniform character and spirit pervade all the legends, making it probable that Fabius and Cincius, as well as Naevius and Ennius, when they began to write, found a ready-made tradition, with fixed popular notions about the principal events of the old period, and moreover a vast number of names and dates, round which the narrative was grouped in a generally accredited digest. How shall we account for the existence of such a popular, unwritten history at the time of the first attempts at historical composition? *[margin: Scarcity of fiction pure and simple.]* *[margin: Existence of a traditional story before Fabius.]*

It was one of Niebuhr's favourite theories that a great portion of the traditional history, embodied in their works by the first annalists, was derived from national epic poetry. Cato and Varro refer to a custom which, they say, prevailed among their ancestors, of singing the praises of great men at festive banquets to an accompaniment of the flute. But we cannot form the slightest conception of the character of these songs. We do not even know whether they were epic or lyric; we are not informed that they were made use of by any of the annalists; and what is a still more decisive objection, the character of the writings of the annalists is eminently dry and unpoetical, with very few exceptions. After all, if Niebuhr's theory were true, it would prove that no reliance could be placed on the alleged poetical stories, for poetry, though it may be based on fact, contains so large an element of fiction, and combines truth and fiction so intimately, that no critical test will enable us to extract from it genuine historical truth.

<small>Non-existence of a national epos.</small>

In the absence of epic poems, which might explain the preservation of the facts of ancient Roman history, we are thrown back upon ordinary oral tradition. This alone, as we have seen, unaided by some external and artificial mode of recording facts, is sure to degenerate very soon. What, for example, would be our notions at the present day of the Revolution of the seventeenth century, if we had to derive our knowledge of it through oral tradition alone? But, it may be objected, we neglect oral tradition because we do not require it in our literary age. There is considerable weight in this objection. The Romans, in the ages before the application of the art of writing to literature, were no doubt compelled to cultivate tradition, if they wished to preserve the memory of the past, and we may give them credit for this from what we know of their national pride. Moreover, the constitution of Rome, like that of England, as we

<small>Oral tradition.</small>

<small>Importance of the knowledge of precedents and customary laws.</small>

have pointed out already, was never subverted entirely by revolutions which swept away the existing institutions and obliterated the memory of the past. All the laws that were in force at any particular time had their roots in previous phases of the commonwealth. Precedents were of much value in deciding questions of the day, and it was necessary for public men to be familiar to a certain extent with the history of previous legislation and the events and conditions which brought it about.

This familiarity with the deeds of their forefathers was greatly facilitated in Rome by the fixity of the Roman families, by the composition of the senate, and by the organization of the priestly bodies.

Of the fostering care given to the memory of their ancestors by the great families of Rome, we shall have to speak by-and-by. The senate, as we shall see, consisted of men chosen for life. It was never wholly renewed. It never died. It contained all the men who had served the state from their youth upwards in peace and war, who were familiar with the laws, and consequently with the history of their people. In their debates previous events must have been constantly referred to; and though the past naturally slips by degrees into the background of memory, yet such startling events as the Gallic invasion, or the conquest of Veii, or the secession of the plebeians, or the legislation of the decemvirs, could never be entirely forgotten.

The senate as conservator of the memory of the past.

Still more preservative of the memories of the past were necessarily those 'collegia' or corporations of priests, who, like the augurs, were intimately connected with every public transaction, or who, like the pontiffs, were the keepers and expositors of all divine and human law. The pontiffs, as we shall presently see, were especially charged with keeping

The sacerdotal corporations.

a public register of important passing events, and although these registers contained probably not so much political as sacerdotal information, respecting temples, omens, or other such matters, yet it is not unlikely that the college of pontiffs was the first to work up and digest into a consecutive narrative the various isolated facts which had been transmitted from preceding times in one way or another, and that the men who took a leading part in public affairs were more or less familiar with a current narrative generally believed to be the history of the Roman people.

<small>Probability of a pontifical narrative.</small>

Nevertheless we cannot imagine that tradition alone would have sufficed to produce a continuous and connected narrative of the transactions of several centuries, however faithfully it might preserve the memory of great national events and eminent public men. The Roman annalists gave year by year the names of the consuls, often men of no great repute, and related many events which are anything but striking or picturesque. Tradition alone would not be able to preserve such a string of names unbroken and unentangled for a great number of years. It would, however, be pushing doubt too far if we were to look upon all those names and stories as fictitious. Moreover the chronological order in which they are related, though sometimes interrupted and sometimes confused, is after all not so hopelessly irregular or contradictory as to be irreconcileable with the natural and probable development of Roman affairs. Its very irregularities, the blanks and contradictions it contains, are in its favour. Were it a deliberate fabrication, it would be much more smooth and plausible. It produces on the whole the impression of a genuine though very imperfect record. To strengthen this confidence, we must enquire whether any such genuine records existed at the time

<small>Oral tradition alone insufficient to account for the detail of the annals.</small>

when the annalists began to write, and what is their character and trustworthiness.

It was an ancient custom at Rome, continued down to the time of the Gracchi (131 B.C.), for the Pontifex Maximus, the head of the pontifical college or corporation, to write down every year the most remarkable events and to publish them on wooden tablets for the information of the people. These tablets were preserved in the *Regia*, the official dwelling of the chief pontiff, near the temple of Vesta on the Roman forum. The attention of the sacerdotal chroniclers, it is true, was directed not so much to political transactions as to occurrences which were looked upon as manifestations of the divine will, such as dearth, famine, pestilence, inundations, earthquakes, and eclipses of the sun and moon. The anger of the gods on such occasions was averted by expiatory sacrifices which the pontiffs prescribed. It is not unlikely that foreign wars and civil disturbances may likewise have been noticed in these annual registers, and at any rate it would seem that to fix the date of any entries the names of the chief magistrates must have been given, as the Romans marked the successive years not by numbering them from a fixed era, but by the names of the magistrates of each year.

The pontifical or great annals.

Thus a meagre, but at any rate a trustworthy abstract of the most striking events must have been compiled from the time when these pontifical annals (called also *Annales Maximi*, after the Pontifex Maximus) were first kept. And, if we could trust a statement of Cicero, the custom of keeping such annals would date from the very foundation of Rome.

This, however, we cannot accept as true. For, not to speak of the regal period, the annals of the republic during the first two centuries exhibit so many discrepancies and contradictions in the names of the annual magistrates, so many repetitions, so many gaps and palpable errors, that the idea of their being based on contemporary evidence is altogether inadmissible. We are driven to the conclusion that the pontifical annals are not of the antiquity assigned to them by Cicero, or that the older ones had been lost when the annalists began to write.

Age of the pontifical annals.

Now this inference is borne out by external evidence. Livy relates, that in the Gallic conflagration most of the public and private records were consumed by the flames. That the pontifical annals were included in this general calamity there can be no doubt, for they were written on wooden tablets, and the hurry of the Romans in their flight was so great that they had difficulty even in saving the sacred fire of Vesta. What could have induced them to burden themselves with these clumsy historical archives, when they could hardly save their bare lives? No room, therefore, is left for doubt that all the contemporaneous records which may have existed before the Gallic war perished at that time, and that the books given out at a later period as copied from the pontifical annals must have been compiled afterwards from memory or from other sources.

Other materials for the oldest annals existed in the shape of various official documents, books of law based on precedents, books containing rules and regulations for different public functionaries, census lists, and, above all, official lists of the annual magistrates. Some of these books may have been kept in the Capitol, which resisted the onset of the Gauls. But the greater part of them must have been renewed after the war, and therefore they cannot claim to be considered unimpeachable contemporary evidence.

Other public documents.

Another kind of documents which may have helped to preserve the memory of bygone times consists of laws and treaties cut in stone or engraved on metal tablets. Among the most important of these were the laws of the twelve tables, which are said to have been exhibited in the Forum. Copper at that time had the value of money; it is therefore not likely that these tablets escaped the rapacity of the Gauls, who whilst they besieged the Capitol ransacked all Rome for hidden treasures. We may be sure that the twelve tables of the Decemvirs did not escape; but as they contained the fundamental laws of the republic, we may be equally sure that they were speedily restored, and moreover that they were restored faithfully. *Laws and treaties. Laws of the twelve tables.*

The same authenticity cannot be attributed to the so-called Laws of the Kings (*leges regiae*), which are often mentioned by later writers and unhesitatingly assigned to one or another of the seven kings as their author. They are all of a more or less religious character, are no doubt of great antiquity, and refer to those rites and religious customs which precede all secular legislation. As the Roman kings were not only civil magistrates, but more emphatically the high priests of the nation, these laws were supposed to have been enacted by them; but they appear never to have been committed to writing in any authoritative form by order of the State, and if any collection existed in the Gallic war, its testimony would have no value as to events of the regal period. *Apocryphal laws of the kings.*

Several ancient writers have left us descriptions of monuments of the primeval age of Rome, including statues of kings and heroes and relics of various kinds, such as the augural staff of Romulus, his straw-thatched hut, the fig tree at the roots of which Faustulus found the basket which contained Romulus and Remus. The value of such pretended documents of *Legendary relics.*

antiquity will not be rated high even in an age in which relics not less wonderful abound and are venerated by thousands. The Romans were as childlike in their craving for the wonderful as our own superstitious classes, and this craving was amply satisfied by priestly and antiquarian craft. Hence, though genuine monuments may preserve the memory of historical events, it is clear that not much of trustworthy history can have been elicited from the objects just enumerated.

Of a very different value, no doubt, are public monuments which contain inscriptions, provided that the age of the monuments and the genuineness of the inscriptions are beyond doubt. But the statues of the Roman kings on the Capitol contained no inscriptions, and the inscriptions on columns and shields which writers like Livy and Dionysius refer to as genuine, can be shown to be fabrications of comparatively recent times.

<small>Public monuments.</small>

We have now reviewed in succession the different sources from which the materials employed by the first annalists of Rome may be supposed to have been drawn. We have found them all very scanty, and it will go hard for the credibility of the early annals if we cannot discover any other sources more copious and clear.

Reference has already been made to the solid structure of the Roman families. The Romans are the only people of antiquity where all families were regularly designated by and propagated under a permanent family name. Whereas in Greece names as a rule were simply designations of individuals, and a man would show that he belonged to a particular family only by adding his father's name to his own, seldom using a patronymic, the Romans had but a very small number of individual, personal names; but everyone bore the name of that particular family to

<small>Fixity and continuity of the Roman families.</small>

which he belonged, such as Horatius, Valerius, Fabius, and the like. The families, not the individual citizens, formed the units of which the Roman people was made up. Each family was a small community in itself, organized for economic and social purposes under the government of the 'paterfamilias,' who had power of life and death, and was the sole owner of the family property as long as he lived. The family dwelt under the same roof often long after the sons were married: its members cultivated in common the family estate, and they were bound to each other by the strongest ties of mutual duty and interest.

The aristocratic spirit which pervades all Roman history is derived from the position and influence which the great families, so firmly and permanently organized, exercised in public affairs. They had existed in isolation and independence before they combined to form a federal community; and they retained a great portion of their original spirit ever afterwards. Religion lent her aid to strengthen this spirit. Adhering strictly in this respect to the earliest form of Aryan civilisation, every family had its own peculiar deity, its family altar, and its family grave. No stranger was allowed to share in the worship of the family, or to be laid in the family tomb. The strictness with which strangers were excluded from the inner communion of a family was proportioned to the strength of the attachment which bound the members together, and the veneration felt by all for the head of the family was transferred to his memory after his death. His grave was a sacred spot, and annual offerings were made to his spirit. Nor was his memory allowed to fall into oblivion. Not only was it the practice for the son to add the father's name to his own, and to call himself, for instance, Lucius Manlius, the son of Marcus

Their aristocratic spirit and pride.

(M. f.), but he added the grandfather's name as well. And those families which could boast of a distinguished progenitor who had served the State in one of the higher places of trust, preserved a bust or rather mask of the departed in the *atrium*, or great hall of the house, and registered his name and the titles of the offices he had filled. Thus the walls of the atrium were filled by degrees with a gallery of family portraits which formed a kind of pedigree, and were the boast and pride of the survivors.

Family portraits.

When a member of the family died, the niches in which the masks were kept were opened. Persons dressed in the official robes of the departed placed the masks before their faces, and thus representing the members of the former generations of the family accompanied the body of the recently deceased to the market-place. There the eldest son or some other member of the family ascended the pulpit and delivered a funeral oration in which he set forth the dead man's virtues and services. Nor did he limit himself to the deeds of one ancestor; but ascending the stream of history he traced the great men of his house to the earlier days of the republic, and dwelt upon their exploits. Such speeches, technically called 'laudations,' kept alive the memory not only of the doings of one family, but of the whole people; they were a kind of popular history viewed from the standpoint of a single family. And as each noble house contributed its share, the smaller streams of family histories naturally united and formed a broad channel of national traditions.

Solemn funerals.

Funeral orations.

The frequent occurrence of such solemnities would naturally suggest the advisability of putting down in writing the leading features of these laudations, for the purpose of assisting the memory and enabling successive speakers to do full justice to those

Written laudations.

whom they were called upon to honour. Thus arose family chronicles, which, as we are distinctly informed, were kept in some noble houses, but which we may safely infer, were common in all. They were preserved in the *tablinum*, the place for the family archives, and they most likely formed the chief written materials from which Fabius and Cincius composed the first national annals.

Family chronicles.

We do not know the precise age when these family chronicles were first composed, nor can we speak with more certainty of the time of the first written laudations. Even the antiquity of the solemn funerals is not attested by any external evidence. But there is nothing to prevent us from supposing that the practice of the solemn funerals, including the laudations, was as old as the republic, and that the first written memorials of the family worthies were made as soon as the art of writing was applied to practical use in public and private life, *i.e.* in the earliest ages of the republic. It is true we must admit that all such memorials which existed at the time of the Gallic war, perished in the flames, except those which may have been preserved in houses on the Capitoline hill. But after the restoration of the city we may be quite sure that most of what had been lost was restored, and restored from a memory which had been constantly refreshed by the periodical recurrence of the occasions for delivering laudatory speeches. Perfect accuracy, of course, was out of the question. Errors of various kinds would creep in, and would be perpetuated. Apart from such involuntary errors, the family traditions would be corrupted by wilful falsifications, by concealing disasters, by exaggerating successes, by repetitions and omissions of various kinds. It is admitted by Cicero that the history of Rome has suffered in veracity from

Their antiquity

and character.

such private documents, and this defect is indeed palpable on the very face of it. But what we contend for is this, that the substratum of all these tales is real and not simply fictitious, that many of the errors can be detected and corrected, and that, even where the detail is lost, the general character of the events and the leading features stand out with sufficient distinctness.

A patient examination of the early annals of Rome shows clearly that their origin from family chronicles is undeniable. The number of noble families sharing among themselves the high offices of state was so small that sometimes for years together the same names occur in the lists of consuls, and so the history of these men is identical with the history of the republic. Thus the Valerii and the Fabii at one time, the Furii and Manlii at another, practically ruled the state and filled the annals with their names. If we assume that the lists of magistrates, imperfectly kept or preserved, but still preserved in some way, enabled the first compilers to reduce the varied and often conflicting statements of the family chronicles to some sort of order; that the memorials in the hands of the pontiffs and other priests and magistrates supplied materials of another kind; that oral tradition enlivened and diversified the dry outline, giving flesh and blood to the skeleton of names and figures; and that a little imagination and editorial skill smoothed down the rough parts of this heterogeneous mass, we can perfectly understand the genesis of the history of primeval Rome, we can account for every peculiar feature which marks it, and we shall wonder no longer at its defects, nor doubt the possibility of its trustworthiness in the general outlines.

<small>General character of the earliest annals.</small>

What we have just said with regard to the origin of

the early annals applies strictly only to those of the republic, and **not to** the so-called history of the Roman kings. This follows as a natural consequence from the fact, that hardly one of the names of families which occur in the republican annals is found in the stories of the regal period. It is clear that the family traditions did not go further back than the establishment of annual chief magistrates. The yearly registers **too**, whatever **may** have been their value, did not include the period anterior to the establishment of the republic. The narrative of the kings passes **over** long periods **of** years in total silence, **whereas the republican** annals give in every year at least the names of the consuls and generally make mention of some political or warlike transaction. **There** is, moreover, another fundamental difference. **The republican annals, it is true,** contain many improbabilities and some statements which **are** altogether incredible; but **on** the whole they **are** sober and keep within the bounds **of** what is possible and credible. The story of the kings, on the other hand, is unreal and improbable from beginning to **end.** Its whole plan, composition, and arrangement **bear the stamp of** bold and clumsy fiction. We **have said above** that internal probability **is not in itself a proof of the** historical truth of a narrative, **for fiction may** be made to resemble truth very closely. But if fiction is so childish and silly that **it cannot be** reconciled with what we all recognise as being in accordance with physical or moral laws, no **amount of** external attestation could make us accept it **as truth.**

Family traditions confined to the republican period.

Different treatment of the regal and the republican period in the annals.

Hence, **in the** absence **of** external evidence, we must apply the test of internal probability **and** possibility to the narrative **of** the kings of Rome. We must therefore make ourselves acquainted with so much of it as will supply us with materials for our criticism. We shall do this the more willingly as, apart from any historical value, the story of Romulus and his successors has a certain degree of literary importance for us. It was believed almost implicitly by the Romans themselves; it furnished their poets and orators with materials for declamation and ornament; it forms part of the knowledge considered essential even now for a good education; and it will serve us as a background for the picture which we shall afterwards draw of the events more justly entitled to our attention and study.

Reasons for noticing the legends of the kings.

CHAPTER III.

THE LEGENDS OF THE SEVEN KINGS OF ROME.

AT the time when the Capitoline and the neighbouring hills were covered with wood or pasture, all the country round about and all the cities of Latium were governed by the kings of the mighty city of Alba Longa, which stood on the banks of the Alban Lake, high on a hill overlooking the whole plain as far as the sea. The city of Alba was built by Ascanius, the son of Aeneas, the Trojan, who had escaped from the burning of Troy, and after many wanderings and adventures had settled on the coast of Latium, and there had built the town of Lavinium. After the death of Aeneas, his son had transferred the seat of his kingdom to Alba, and there his descendants ruled for 300 years in prosperity and peace.

The legend of Aeneas the Trojan.

Now when the time was fulfilled in which, according to the decree of the gods, Rome should be built, it came to pass that after the death of Procas, the King of Alba, a quarrel arose between his two sons for the throne. Amulius, the younger, took the government from his elder brother Numitor, killed his son, and made his daughter, Rhea Silvia a priestess of Vesta, to the end that she should remain a virgin all her life, engaged in the service of the goddess who presides over the city hearth and loves purity and chastity in those who serve her. But the wicked king was not able to oppose the will of the gods. For Mars, the god of war, loved the virgin, and she bore twins. When Amulius heard this, he ordered the mother to be killed and the twins to be thrown into the river Tiber. But the gods watched over the children, and the basket in which they were laid floated to the foot of the Palatine hill near the cave of the god Lupercus, and was caught by the branches of a fig-tree. The waters of the river now fell rapidly, and the twins were left upon the land.

Birth of Romulus and Remus.

Attracted by their cry, a she-wolf came out from the cave of Lupercus and suckled them with her own milk and licked them with her tongue. When Faustulus, a shepherd who tended his flocks hard by, saw this, he scared away the animal and brought the children to his wife Larentia, and called them Romulus and Remus, and brought them up as his own children. Thus the boys grew up among the shepherds, and they distinguished themselves by their strength and courage, and protected the weak against the lawless men who went forth to pillage and plunder. Then it came to pass that their enemies fell upon them while they were celebrating the festival of the god Pan. Remus was taken prisoner and brought before his grandfather Numitor, and accused of having injured his cattle. But Romulus escaped. Now Faustulus delayed no longer, but told Romulus of his mother, and how he was destined to death by Amulius, and miraculously saved. So Romulus and his followers forced their way into the town of Alba, and set his brother free, and the two brothers having slain the unjust and cruel Amulius, placed their grandfather Numitor again upon the throne.

But the brothers would not remain in Alba, and determined to build a new city on one of the seven hills by the Tiber, near the spot where they had grown up among the shepherds, and they were joined by many from Alba and from the whole country of the Latins.

Now as Romulus and Remus were twins, and as neither would yield to the other in honour and power, *Dispute between Romulus and Remus.* a quarrel arose between them and their followers which of them should give his name to the new town and govern it. And they determined to let the gods decide by a sign from the sacred birds. Then Romulus with his followers observed the heavens from the Palatine hill, and Remus took his station on the Aventine, and thus they both waited for a sign from heaven, from midnight until morning. Then there appeared to Remus six vultures, and he rejoiced and sent messengers to his brother announcing that the gods had decided in his favour. But at the same moment Romulus saw twelve vultures, and it was plain that the gods gave the preference to Romulus. Therefore he built *Building of Rome by Romulus.* the town on the Palatine hill and called it Rome, after his own name, and drew a furrow round it with the sacred plough, and along by the furrow he built a wall and dug a trench. But when Remus saw the doings of his brother, he mocked him, and leaped over the wall and the trench to show him *Death of Remus.* how easily the town might be taken. Then Romulus was wroth and slew his brother, saying, 'Thus perish everyone who may attempt to cross these walls.' And this remained a warning word for all future times, that no enemy should venture to attack Rome unpunished.

After this, Romulus, to increase the number of his people, opened a place of refuge on the Capitoline hill. And there came a great many robbers and fugitives of all kinds from all the surrounding nations, and Romulus received them all and protected them and made them citizens of his town. *The asylum of Romulus.*

But there was a lack of women in the new community. Therefore Romulus sent messengers to the towns round about, asking the neighbours to give their daughters in marriage to the Romans. But the messengers were sent back with scorn and charged to say, that there could be no union and no friendship with a band of robbers and outcasts. When Romulus heard this answer, he hid his anger and invited the dwellers round about to come to Rome with their wives and children to see the games which the Romans wished to celebrate in honour of the god Consus; and there came a great number of Sabines who lived in the city of Cures among the mountains. Now when all eyes were fixed on the games, suddenly a number of armed Romans rushed forward and carried away the young women of the Sabines. After this the parents of the women hurried away from Rome, cursing the faithless town and vowing that they would take vengeance on Romulus and his people. When they had returned home, they gathered a great army and placed Titus Tatius their king at their head, and marched down the valley of the Tiber until they reached the Quirinal hill. There they pitched their camp and laid siege to the Capitoline hill, which was held by the Romans. Now, one day when Tarpeia, the daughter of the Roman captain, had gone out to draw water, the Sabines begged her to open a gate *Rape of the Sabines.*

Tarpeia.

and to let them into the citadel. Tarpeia promised to do this, and made them swear to give her what they wore on their left arms, meaning thereby their gold armlets and rings; whereupon when the Sabines had penetrated into the citadel, they threw their heavy shields which they wore on their left arms on Tarpeia and killed her with the weight. So the traitress met with her reward.

Now when the Sabines had won the Capitol, they fought with the Romans who lived on the Palatine, and the battle raged up and down in the valley which separates the two hills. One day, when Hostus Hostilius, a foremost champion of the Romans, had fallen, his countrymen were seized with fear, and turned to flight. But at the gate of the town Romulus stopped, raised his hands to heaven, and vowed to build on this spot a temple dedicated to Jupiter Stator, that is, the Stayer of Flight, if he would be helpful to the Romans in this need. Then, as if a voice from heaven had commanded them, the Romans stayed their flight, turned round upon the Sabines, and drove them back. And it came to pass that Mettius Curtius, the leader of the Sabines, sank with his horse into the marsh which covered the lower part of the valley, and almost perished in the marsh. And the place where this happened was called for ever after the Lake of Curtius.

War of the Romans and Sabines.

Mettius Curtius.

When the battle had come to a standstill, and Romans and Sabines were facing each other ready to begin the fight afresh, the Sabine women rushed between the combatants, praying their fathers and brothers on the one side, and their husbands on the other, to end the bloody strife, or to turn their arms against them who were the cause of the slaughter. Then the men listened to the voice of the women; and the chiefs on each side came forward and consulted together, and made peace, and, to put an end to all disputes for ever, they agreed to make one people of the Romans and Sabines, and to live peaceably together as citizens of one town. Thus the Sabines remained in Rome, the city was doubled in size and in the number of inhabitants, and **Titus Tatius, the** Sabine king, reigned jointly with Romulus. But as Tatius and his people came from Cures, the city of the Sabines, high up among the mountains, the united people were called the ' Roman people and **the Quirites,'** and the name remained in use for all **times.** *Union of the Romans and the Sabines.*

After a time **Tatius** had a quarrel with the men of Laurentum, who slew him when he was bringing offerings to the sanctuary of the Penates at Lavinium. Thenceforward Romulus reigned alone over the two **peoples,** and he made laws to govern them in peace and war; and first of all he divided them into nobles and commons; **the nobles he called** Patricians and the commons Plebeians. Then he divided the Patricians into three tribes, **the Ramnes,** the Tities, and the Luceres, and in each of these tribes he made ten divisions, which he called Curies. **And the** thirty **Curies** together formed **the assembly of the people, and** met to administer justice **and to make laws.** But all the patricians were equal among themselves, **and every father of a** family governed those of his own house, **his** wife, his children, and his slaves, with absolute **power over life** and death. And several families **united together** and formed houses, and the houses had their own sanctuaries, customs, **and laws.** But the plebeians **Romulus** portioned **out as** tenants and dependants among the patricians, **and called** them Clients, and commanded **them to serve their** masters faithfully and **to help them** in peace and in war; and the patricians he **recommended to** protect their clients against injustice; and **on that account** he called them *The laws of Romulus.*

Patrons, that is, Protectors. From among the patricians, again, he chose a hundred of the oldest and wisest men, whom he called **Fathers,** and made them his council to advise him on all great matters of state and to help him to govern the city in time of peace. But out of the young men he chose a legion or army of 3,000 foot soldiers, and 300 horse, according to the number of the three tribes and the thirty curies, out of every curia 100 foot soldiers and ten horsemen, and for the captain of the horsemen he chose a tribune of the Celeres (for this was the name of the horsemen).

After the city had been so ordered and made strong to defend her freedom, Romulus governed wisely and justly for many years, and was beloved by his people as a father. He overcame his enemies in many wars, and conquered **Fidenae,** an Etruscan town on the left bank of the Tiber, not far from Rome.

Now when all that Romulus had to carry out was fulfilled according to the will of the gods, it came to pass that he assembled the people to a festival of atonement at the Goat-pool, on the field of Mars, which extends from the town towards the north even to the Tiber. Then there arose suddenly a fearful storm, and the sun was darkened, and out of the clouds came lightning, and the earth quaked with the thunder. And the people were frightened and waited anxiously till the storm should clear away. But when daylight returned, Romulus had disappeared and was nowhere to be found. *Death of Romulus.* And his people mourned for him. Then Proculus Julius, an honourable man, came forward and said that Romulus had appeared to him as a god, bidding him tell his people to worship him as Quirinus, and to practise valour and all warlike virtues, that they might please him and might gain for themselves the power over all other nations. Then the Romans rejoiced and erected on the Quirinal hill an altar to the god Quirinus, and worshipped him as their national hero and their protector for ever.

When Romulus had left the earth and had become a god, the Fathers met together and appointed intermediate kings from the senate, to reign in turn each for five days, in the place of the king, till a new king should be chosen. This temporary government or interregnum lasted a whole year; for the Romans were at variance with the Sabines, and quarrelled about the choice of the new king. At last they agreed that a Sabine should be taken, but that the Romans should choose him. *(The first interregnum.)*

There lived at that time in the land of the Sabines a righteous man called Numa Pompilius, who was honoured and beloved by everyone on account of his wisdom and piety. This man the Romans chose to be king over Rome. And when Numa was assured of the consent of the gods by the flight of the sacred birds, he called together an assembly of the thirty Curies, and asked them whether they would willingly obey all his commands. Then the people consented, and Numa reigned in Rome forty-three years until his death. *(Numa Pompilius, the second king.)*

Now the Romans were a rude people: their thoughts were intent on war and plunder, and with them might went before right. Therefore Numa was grieved, for he wished to accustom the people to milder habits and the fear of the gods, and to curb their spirit by the sacred laws of religion. But the people would not believe him and mocked him. Then he prepared a simple meal, and invited guests to his house, and placed before them plain food on earthen plates and water in stone bottles. And when they sat down to eat suddenly all the dishes were changed into silver and gold, *(His sacred laws.)*

and the plain food into choice viands and the water into wine. Then everyone knew that a divine power dwelt in Numa, and they were willing to receive his statutes. And Numa was wise from his youth upwards, as a sign of which his hair was grey from his birth, and he was trained in all the wisdom of the Greeks; for Pythagoras, the wisest of the Greeks, had instructed him; and Egeria, a Camena, that is a Muse, taught him the worship of the gods and the duties of a pious life. And once he deceived Faunus and Picus, the prophesying gods of the wood, by wine which he poured into the spring from which they drank; and he intoxicated them and bound them, till they told him the secret charms by which they compelled Jupiter to reveal his will.

Thus Numa was full of all wisdom, and taught the people which gods they should worship and what sacred rites they should perform to obtain their favour. And all bloody offerings he forbade, permitting only simple cakes and milk and other like offerings to be presented to the gods. Nor would he allow any images to be made of the gods, for he taught the people to believe that the gods had no bodies, and that as pure spirits they pervaded all nature and watched over the destiny of men. Moreover he taught the people what prayers, solemn words, and ceremonies they should employ in all transactions of public and private life; and he ordained that they should not undertake anything important without first calling on the gods and seeking their favour.

Then Numa instituted priests to Jupiter, Mars, and Quirinus. And for the service of Vesta he chose pure virgins who should feed the sacred flame on her altar, the common hearth of the city. Also, in order to discover the will of the gods, he instituted the office of augurs, and instructed them in the science of the flight of the sacred birds. And he appointed many more priests and servants of the altars, and prescribed to each what he should do; and, that they might all know what was right in the service of the gods, and not from ignorance employ the wrong prayers, or leave out or neglect any rite whereby they might incur the anger of the gods and suffer great punishment, Numa wrote all his statutes in a book, and handed it over to Numa Marcius, whom he made chief 'pontifex,' that is, overseer and watcher over the service of the gods.

Moreover Numa encouraged the peaceful arts, that the people might live by the produce of their labour, and not think of robbing others. For this purpose he divided among the citizens the land which Romulus had conquered, and bade them cultivate it; and he consecrated the stones which marked the boundaries of the fields, and erected an altar on the Capitoline hill to Terminus, the god of boundaries. *His civil laws.*

In the same manner he took care of all artizans in the town who possessed no land. He divided them into guilds and set masters over them according to each kind of trade; and in order that truth and good faith might be practised in common intercourse, and that promises might be kept as sacred as oaths, he founded the service of the goddess Fides, that is Faith, and built a temple to her on the Capitol.

While Numa was thus occupied with works of peace, the weapons of war lay idle, and the neighbouring people were afraid of disturbing the tranquillity of this righteous king. So the gates of the temple of Janus remained closed, for it was the custom among the Romans to open them only in time of war. *The peace of Numa.*

Thus the reign of Numa was a time of peace and happiness, and the gods testified their pleasure in the pious king and his people; for they guarded the country from sickness and dearth, and blessed and prospered all that the people undertook.

Now when Numa had become old and weak, he died without illness and pain, and the Romans mourned for him as for a father, and buried him on the hill Janiculus beyond the Tiber, on that side which lies towards the west.

After Numa's death the Romans chose for their king **Tullus Hostilius,** the grandson of Hostus Hostilius, who fought in the battle with the Sabine, Mettius Curtius. The time of peace was now at an end, for Tullus was not like Numa, but like Romulus, and he loved war and the glory of war beyond everything. Therefore he sought causes of dispute among the neighbours, for he thought that in a long peace the Romans would grow effeminate and lose their ancient courage.

<small>Tullus Hostilius, the third king.</small>

Just then it happened that some Roman and Alban countrymen quarrelled and charged each the other with robbery. Therefore Tullus sent 'fetiales,' or heralds, to Alba, to demand compensation for the plunder. The Albans likewise sent messengers to Rome to complain and to insist on justice.

<small>War with Alba.</small>

Then Tullus employed a stratagem. He received the Alban messengers with great kindness and treated them with such hospitality that they delayed the execution of their disagreeable commission. But the Roman fetiales, who were sent to Alba, demanded without delay satisfaction from the Albans, and when this was refused they declared war in the name of the Roman people. When Tullus heard this, he asked the Alban ambassadors to deliver their message, and sent them home without giving satisfaction, because the Albans had first refused it, and had thus provoked an unjust war. Now the Romans and Albans met in the field. The Albans, led by their king Cluilius, encamped with their army on the frontier of the Roman territory, and made a deep trench round their camp. And the trench was called, for ever after, the 'trench of Cluilius.' But in the following night the king of the Albans died; and they chose in his place a dictator, whose name was Mettius Fufetius.

Now, when Tullus advanced, and the two armies stood arrayed against one another, and the bloody fight between the kindred nations was about to begin, the leaders came forward and consulted together, *The Horatii and Curiatii.* and determined to decide the war by a single combat of Albans and Romans, lest too much blood should be spilt. There were by chance in the Roman army three brothers born at one birth, and likewise in the Alban army three brothers born at one birth. These were the sons of twin sisters, and equal in age and strength. Therefore they were chosen as the combatants, and the Romans and Albans bound themselves by an oath that the nation whose champions should be victorious should rule over the other. Then began the fight between the three Horatii, the champions of the Romans, and the three Curiatii, the champions of the Albans. On the first onset two of the Horatii fell, and the three Curiatii were wounded. Then the surviving Horatius took to flight and the Curiatii pursued him. But he turned suddenly round and killed the one of the three who was the most slightly wounded and had hurried on before the others. Then he ran towards the second and conquered him also, and at last he killed the third, who, on account of his wounds, was able to pursue him but very slowly. Then the Romans rejoiced and welcomed Horatius as conqueror, and they collected the spoils of the slain Curiatii and carried them before Horatius and led him in triumph to Rome.

When the procession came near the gate of the city, the sister of Horatius went forth to meet it. She was betrothed to one of the Curiatii who had been killed. And when she saw the bloody coat of her lover, which she herself had embroidered, she sobbed and moaned, and cursed her brother. At this Horatius fell into a violent rage, and drew his sword and stabbed his sister to the heart, because she had wept over a fallen enemy. But the blood of the slain sister called for vengeance, and Horatius was accused before the criminal judges, who sentenced him to death. The people, however, rejected the sentence of the judges out of compassion for the aged father of Horatius, who had lost three of his children in one day, and because they would not see the man led to death who had ventured his life for the greatness of his country, and had gained the victory over Alba with his own hand. But to atone for his crime Horatius had to do public penance, to pass under a yoke, and to offer up expiatory sacrifices to the spirit of his murdered sister. The beam of the yoke under which Horatius passed remained as a token to the latest times and was called the 'sister beam.' But the memory of the heroism of Horatius was also preserved; and the arms of the Curiatii were hung up on a pillar in the forum; and the pillar was called the 'pillar of Horatius' for all time.

<small>Crime of Horatius.</small>

Thus Alba became subject to Rome, and the Albans were obliged to help the Romans in their wars. But Mettius Fufetius, the dictator of the Albans, meditated treason and hoped to overthrow the power of Rome. Therefore when war had broken out between the Romans and the Etruscans of Fidenae and Veii, and when the Romans and Albans were drawn up against the enemy, and the battle was raging fiercely, Mettius kept his army back from the fight, and hoped that the Romans would be subdued. But Tullus, perceiving the treason, bade his soldiers be of good courage,

<small>Treason of Mettius.</small>

and conquered the Etruscans. And when Mettius came to him after the battle to wish him joy on account of the victory, thinking that Tullus had not discovered his treachery, Tullus ordered him to be seized and torn to pieces by horses, as a punishment for wavering in his fidelity between the Romans and their enemies. Then the Albans were disarmed, and Tullus sent horsemen to Alba, who burned the whole town, with the exception of the temples, and led the inhabitants away to Rome. From that time Alba Longa was desolate; but the Albans became Roman citizens, and their nobles were received among the patricians, so that Albans and Romans became one people, as the Romans and the Sabines had become in the reign of Romulus. *Destruction of Alba.*

After this, Tullus waged many wars with his neighbours, the Etruscans and the Sabines, and he became proud and haughty, neglecting the gods and their service, and regarding not justice and the laws of Numa. Therefore the gods sent a plague among the people, and at last they smote him also with a sore disease. Then he became aware that he had sinned, and he sought to find out the will of Jupiter, according to the spells of Numa. But Jupiter was wroth, and struck him with lightning, and destroyed his house so that no trace was left behind. Thus ended Tullus Hostilius after he had been king for thirty-two years; and Ancus Marcius, the grandson of Numa Pompilius, was chosen king in his stead. *Tullus's wickedness and death.*

Ancus was a just and peaceful man, who made it his first care to restore in its purity the service of the gods. For this reason he caused the sacred laws of Numa to be written on wooden tablets, and to be exhibited before the people; and he endeavoured to preserve peace and the peaceful arts as *Ancus Marcius, the fourth king.*

Numa had done, whose example he wished to follow in all things.

But it was not vouchsafed to him always to avoid war. For when the Latins heard that Tullus was dead, and that in his stead reigned a peace-loving king, who passed his time quietly at home in prayer and sacrifice, they made a raid into the country of the Romans, and thought to plunder it with impunity. Then Ancus left the management of the public worship to the priests, and took up arms and fought with his enemies, and conquered their towns and destroyed them. And many of the inhabitants he brought to Rome, and gave them dwellings on the Aventine hill. Therefore Ancus enlarged the city, and dug a deep trench in that part where the slope of the hills was not steep enough to protect Rome from her enemies. After this he fortified the hill Janiculus on the right bank of the Tiber, and built a wooden bridge over the river; and he conquered all the land between Rome and the sea, and planted a colony at the mouth of the Tiber, which he called Ostia, and made there a harbour for sea-going ships. And when Ancus had been king for four-and-twenty years he died calmly and happily like Numa, and the Romans honoured his memory, for he was just in time of peace, and vigorous and victorious in war.

War with the Latins.

At the time when Ancus Marcius was king, there lived in the town of Tarquinii, in the land of the Etruscans, a rich and prudent man called Lucumo, the son of Demaratos, a noble of the race of the Bacchiads of Corinth, who had been driven by the tyrant Kypselos out of his native town and had fled to Etruria. Now, because Lucumo was the son of a stranger, the people of Tarquinii disliked him and refused him a place of honour in their town. His wife Tanaquil therefore advised him to leave Tarquinii and to emigrate to Rome,

Lucumo of Tarquinii.

where strangers were kindly received. Thereupon Lucumo set out for Rome. When he had come to the hill Janiculus, near the town, an eagle shot down from the air and took his hat from his head and flew away with it; and after wheeling about for a time over the carriage in which Lucumo and his wife Tanaquil sat, the bird flew down again and replaced the hat on the head of Lucumo. Then Tanaquil, who knew the heavenly signs, foresaw that her husband was destined to attain high honours in Rome.

Now in Rome, Lucumo altered his name, and called himself Lucius Tarquinius, after his native town, and he was soon highly regarded, for he was wise in council, stout in war, and kind to his inferiors. For this reason King Ancus took him for his counsellor, confided to him the most weighty matters, and before he died made him the guardian of his sons. Then Tarquinius contrived that the people should choose him, and not one of the sons of Ancus, for their king; and thus the divine omen which Tanaquil, his wife, had explained to him, was fulfilled. *Lucius Tarquinius, the fifth king.*

When Tarquinius had become king, he carried on war with the Latins and conquered many of their towns. He made war also on the Sabines, who had invaded the Roman country with a large and powerful army, and had penetrated even to the walls of the city. And when Tarquinius was at war with them and was in great danger, he vowed a temple to Jupiter, and so he overcame his enemies. Then he waged war against the Etruscans, and subdued the whole land of Etruria, so that the Etruscans acknowledged him as their king and sent him a golden crown, a sceptre, an ivory chair, an embroidered tunic, a purple toga, and twelve axes tied up in bundles of rods. Thus the emblems of royal power were brought to Rome, and were *Wars with the Latins and Sabines.*

displayed by the Roman kings as a sign of their dominion over the people.

The reforms of Tarquinius.

When all enemies were conquered, and Rome had increased in power, in size, and in the number of its citizens, Tarquinius determined to make a new division of the people, and to appoint other tribes in the place of the Ramnes, the Tities, and the Luceres, which Romulus had ordained. But the gods sent unfavourable signs, and the augur Attus Navius opposed the king and forbade any alteration of the old division of the people against the will of the gods. Then Tarquinius thought to mock and to humble the augur, and bade him consult the sacred birds, whether what he then purposed in his mind could come to pass. And when Attus Navius had consulted the birds and had obtained an answer that the king's wish should be done, Tarquinius gave him a whetstone and a razor, and said, 'This is what I purposed in my mind; you shall cut through the stone with this knife.' Then Attus cut the stone through with the knife and compelled Tarquinius to give up his intentions. But the knife and the stone were buried in the Forum, and hard by the spot a statue of Attus Navius was set up to commemorate the miracle which he wrought.

As Tarquinius could not alter the name of the old tribes nor increase their number, he doubled the number of the noble houses in each tribe, and called those which he now admitted the younger houses of the Ramnes, the Tities, and the Luceres. He doubled also the number of the knights and of the senate, so that the division of the people which Romulus had made and the old names remained unaltered, except that in each division the number of the houses was doubled.

Now, to fulfil the vow that he had made in the war with the Sabines, Tarquinius began to build a temple to

Jupiter on the Capitoline hill. For this he levelled a place on the hill to lay the foundation of the temple. And as they were digging they found a human head. This was interpreted as a sign that that place should be the head of all the earth. And the old sanctuaries which stood in the place where the temple of Jupiter was to be built were transferred to other places, according to the sacred rites which the pontifices prescribed. But the altars of the god of youth and of the god of boundaries could not be transferred. So they had to be left in their places, and were inclosed in the temple of Jupiter, and this was a sign that the boundary line of the Roman commonwealth should never recede and that its youth would be everlasting. *Temple of Jupiter on the Capitol.*

Moreover Tarquinius built large sewers underground, and drained the lower valleys of the city which lay between the hills, and which till then were marshy and uninhabitable. And in the valley between the Capitoline and the Palatine hills he laid out the forum for a market-place, and surrounded it with covered walks and booths. He drained also the valley of Murcia, between the Aventine and the Palatine, and there he levelled a race-course, and introduced games like those of the Etruscans, which he celebrated every year, and called the 'Roman games.' Thus Tarquinius reigned for thirty-seven years and gained great renown in peace and in war. *The great sewer, forum, and circus*

Among the servants of King Tarquinius was a virgin called Ocrisia, who watched the holy fire sacred to the household god. Once, as she sat by the hearth, the god appeared to her in the flame. After a while she bore him a son, who grew up in the house of the king, and they called him Servius, because he was the son of a slave. One day, when the boy had fallen asleep in a chamber in the king's *Miraculous birth of Servius Tullius.*

house, a flame played about his head till he awoke. And Tanaquil, the king's wife, saw from this that Servius was destined for great things. Therefore, when he was grown up to manhood, Tarquinius gave him his daughter in marriage, and intrusted to him the most important business of state, so that Servius was in the highest repute among the elders, as well as among the people. When this became known to the sons of King Ancus, who were wroth with Tarquinius because he had deprived them of their paternal heritage, they were afraid that Tarquinius would make Servius his successor. Therefore they resolved to have their revenge, and they hired two murderers, who came to the king disguised as shepherds, and said that they had a dispute and that the king should judge between them. Now, as they were wrangling with one another and Tarquinius was attending to what one of them was saying, the other struck him with an axe, and they both took to flight.

While the king lay in his blood, a noise and tumult arose in the town, and Tanaquil ordered the gates of the royal house to be shut, to keep out the people. And she spoke to them out of an upper window, and said that the king was not dead, but only wounded, and had ordered that Servius should reign in his stead until he had recovered. Therefore Servius filled the king's place, and sat as judge on the royal throne, conducting all affairs as the king himself was wont to do. But when it became known, after some days, that Tarquinius had died, Servius did not resign the royal power, but continued to rule for a time, without being appointed by the people and without the consent of the senate. Then after he had won over a large number of the people by all kinds of promises and by grants of land, he held an assembly and persuaded the people to choose him for their king.

Thus Servius Tullius became king of Rome, and he ruled with clemency and justice. He loved peace, like his predecessors Numa and Ancus, and waged no wars, except with the Etruscans. These he compelled to be subject to him, as they had been to King Tarquinius before him. *Servius Tullius, the sixth king.* But with the Latins he made a treaty, that the Romans and the Latins should live always in friendship with one another. And as a sign of this union, the Romans and the Latins built a temple to Diana on the Aventine, where they celebrated their common festivals, and offered up sacrifices every year for Rome and for the whole of Latium.

Then Servius built a strong wall from the Quirinal to the Esquiline, and made a deep trench and added the Esquiline to the town, so that all the seven hills were united and formed one city. This city he divided into four parts, which he called tribes, after the old division of the people; and he divided the land round about the city into twenty-six districts, and ordered common sanctuaries and holy days, and appointed chief men over the inhabitants of the districts which he had made.

Now, as Servius was the son of a bondmaid, he was a friend of the poor and of the lower classes, and he established equitable laws and ordinances to protect the common people against the powerful. Therefore the commons honoured him and called him the good king Servius, and they celebrated the day of his birth as an annual festival. But the greatest work that Servius did was to make a new division of the people, according to the order of the fighting men, as they were arranged in the field of battle, and as they voted in the assembly of citizens when the king consulted them concerning peace or war, or laws, or elections, or other weighty matters.

For this purpose Servius divided the whole people of the patricians and the plebeians into five classes, according to their property, without regard to blood or descent, so that from that time forward the three tribes of Romulus—the Ramnes, the Tities, and the Luceres—and their thirty curies, formed no longer the principal assembly of citizens, but lost their power in most matters that affected the government.

The centuriate assembly of the people

The first class Servius made to consist of forty centuries of the younger men, who were under forty-six years of age, and of forty centuries of the older; the latter for the defence of the town, the former for service in the field. The second, third, and fourth classes he divided each into twenty centuries, ten of the older men and ten of the younger. But he made the fifth class stronger, for he gave it thirty centuries, fifteen of the older men and fifteen of the younger. And the arming of the centuries was not the same in all the five classes, for only the men of the first class wore complete armour, composed of breast-plate, helmet, shield and greaves, with javelin, lance, and sword. The second class fought without the breast-plate and with a lighter shield. The third without the greaves, and so on, so that the men of the fifth class were but lightly armed. Now, as the citizens had to procure their own equipment for war, and as the complete armour was very costly, Servius chose for the first class only the richest citizens whose property was estimated at more than a hundred thousand *asses*, that is pounds of copper. The assessment for each of the following classes was twenty-five thousand *asses* less, so that in the fifth class were those citizens who were assessed at less than twenty-five thousand *asses*. But those who had less than eleven thousand *asses* Servius arranged in no class at all, but made of them a separate century—the century of the Proletarians—and these he exempted from all military service.

Thus Servius arranged the infantry in 170 centuries, and for the horse he took the six double centuries of horsemen which Tarquinius had established, and to them he added twelve new centuries, chosen out of the richest families. The horsemen consisted all of younger men, for they had to fight only in the field.

Moreover, as it was necessary to have trumpeters, armourers, and carpenters in the army, Servius made four centuries of them, so that altogether 193 centuries were formed.

Such was the military order of the people. When they assembled for making laws or for elections, they observed the same order, each century having a vote; and the chief influence was in the hands of the wealthiest, who formed the eighty centuries of the first class, and the eighteen centuries of knights. But the poorer people, although much more numerous, had but few votes. Thus their influence in the assembly was small, and the greatest number had not the greatest power. Nor was this arrangement unjust, for the rich provided themselves with heavy armour and fought in the foremost rank, and when a war tax was laid on, they contributed in proportion to their property. And Servius showed his wisdom especially in this, that in the assembly of citizens he placed the older men and the younger on an equality in the number of their votes, although there were fewer of the older, according to the nature of things. For he wished that the experience and moderation of the older citizens should restrain the rashness of the younger. In this manner the people were arranged as an army for the protection of their country, and at the same time as an assembly of citizens, to decide all matters which concerned the well-being of the city; and no man was entirely shut out from the commonwealth, but to each were assigned such burdens and services as he might be able to bear, and such a measure of rights and privileges as was just. The order of centuries which Servius Tullius had made remained for many ages the foundation of the Roman commonwealth; and although, in the course of time, it was altered in many ways, it was never entirely abolished, so long as the people of Rome retained their freedom.

Servius Tullius had two daughters; of whom one was good and gentle, and the other haughty, imperious, and heartless. In like manner Aruns and Lucius, the two sons of the elder Tarquinius, were of different character; the one was good-tempered, and the other was vicious and violent. These sons of Tarquin Servius Tullius married to his own daughters, and thinking to soften the hearts of the wicked by the gentleness of the good, he gave to the wicked Lucius the sweet Tullia to wife, and the proud Tullia he married to the good-natured Aruns.

Murder of King Servius.

But matters turned out differently from what Servius had expected. The wicked ones longed for each others' company, and they despised their amiable consorts as weak and mean-spirited. Therefore the bad Lucius murdered his wife and his brother, and he took to wife the daughter of Servius who had a like disposition to his own. So the two evil ones were married and excited one another to new enormities, for they desired to possess power, and by practising deceit and cunning they made for themselves a party among the nobles and those of the people who were the enemies of Servius on account of his new laws.

Now when everything was prepared, Lucius Tarquinius entered the market-place clothed in the royal robes, and, surrounded by a band of armed men, summoned the senators to appear before him, and harangued them as king. At the report of this usurpation, Servius was alarmed and hurried to the spot, and there arose a quarrel in the senate-house between him and his son-in-law. Then Tarquinius seized the old man, and cast him down the steps of the senate-house, and sent after him men who overtook him on his way to his own house, and slew him in the street. But the wicked Tullia, the daughter of Servius, full of joy at what had happened, hurried to the market-place in her carriage, and welcomed her husband as king. And as she was returning through the street where her father lay dead, she ordered the driver not to turn the horses aside, but to drive on over the corpse of her father, so that the carriage and her dress were spattered with his blood.

Thus Tarquinius gained the royal power without the consent of the senate, and without the choice of the people; and as he had acquired it so he exercised it, so that the people called him the Haughty, and hated him as long as he lived. *Lucius Tarquinius, the seventh king.* For he regarded not the laws and ordinances of good king Servius, nor did he summon the senate for counsel, but reigned according to his own will, and oppressed the people, both high and low. Moreover, he surrounded himself with a body-guard, after the custom of the Greek tyrants; and those among the citizens who were against him, or whose wealth provoked his avarice, he punished, upon false accusation, either inflicting heavy fines, or driving them into exile, or putting them to death; but the poor he compelled to work at his buildings, and made them serve like slaves beyond their strength, so that many killed themselves out of despair.

After Tarquinius had established his power in Rome,

he turned against the Latins; and on those who would not willingly submit he waged war, and made them subject to himself. But the people of Gabii resisted manfully, and he could not prevail against them. Then his son Sextus devised this stratagem. He went to Gabii, as if he were flying from his father, and showed his back covered with bloody stripes, and begged the people of Gabii, with supplications and tears, to protect him from his father, and to receive him into their town. Thus the people of Gabii were deceived, and they trusted his words, and befriended him, and made him the commander of a company of soldiers. But the Romans fled when Sextus led the men of Gabii, for this had been agreed upon between Sextus and his father. So when Sextus had thus gained the confidence of the Gabine people and had been entrusted with the chief command, he sent a messenger to his father to ask what he should do. The king was walking in his pleasure-grounds when the messenger came, and, instead of giving him an answer in words, he struck off with his stick the tallest poppies and sent the man back. Sextus understood the meaning of his father's reply, and began to bring false charges against the first and noblest of the men of Gabii, and so caused them to be put to death; and when he had done this, he surrendered the helpless town to his father.

Conquest of Gabii.

Now in order to strengthen his power, Tarquinius united himself to Octavius Mamilius, who reigned in Tusculum, and gave him his daughter to wife; and he established the festival of the Latin games, which were solemnised every year, on the Alban hill at the temple of Jupiter Latiaris, for all the Latin cities. After this he waged war on the Volscians, a powerful people who lived in the south of Latium, and conquered Suessa Pometia, their greatest and richest town. With the spoils thus obtained

Establishment of Roman power over Latium.

he finished the temple of Jupiter on the Capitol, which his father had begun, and the great sewers, and the Forum or market-place. He also adorned the town with many other buildings, for he loved pomp and splendour, and he thought by his great extravagance and by compulsory labour to make the people poor and helpless, that he might govern them more easily.

Now, when he was in full possession of power there appeared one day before him a strange woman, who offered for sale nine books of divine prophecies, which the inspired Sibyl of Cumae had written on loose leaves. But, because she asked a high price, Tarquinius laughed at her and let her go. *Purchase of the Sibylline books.* Then the woman burnt three of the books before his eyes, and returned and offered to sell the other six for the same price which she had at first asked for the nine. But Tarquinius laughed at her still more, and thought she was mad. Then she burnt three more of the books, and offered the last three for the original price. Thereupon Tarquinius began to reflect seriously, and he felt persuaded that the woman was sent to him by the gods and he bought the books. In this manner the king obtained the Sibylline prophecies, and he carefully preserved them and appointed two men who knew the language of the Greeks, in which the books were written, to take charge of them, and to consult them in time of great danger, or dearth or pestilence, to the end that the will of the gods might be known, and that their wrath might be averted from the people.

Up to this time Tarquinius had been always fortunate in his undertakings, and he became ever more and more haughty and cruel. But when he had grown old he was frightened by dreams and wonderful signs, and he determined to consult the oracle of the Greeks at Delphi. So he sent his two sons to Delphi, *Message to Delphi.*

and with them Junius, his sister's son, who on account of his silliness was called **Brutus**. But the silliness of Brutus was only assumed to deceive the tyrant, who was an enemy of all wise men, because he feared them. Now when the king's sons brought costly presents to the Delphian god, Brutus gave only a simple staff. His cousins laughed at him, but they did not know that the staff was hollowed out and filled with gold. After they had executed the commission of their father, they asked the god to tell them who would reign in Rome after Tarquinius. And the answer of the oracle was, that he should reign who should first kiss his mother. Then the two brothers agreed to draw lots which of them should first kiss his mother on their return. But Brutus perceived the real meaning of the oracle, and when they had left the temple, he pretended to stumble, and fell down and kissed the ground, for the earth, he thought, was the common mother of all men.

Now when Tarquinius had reigned twenty-four years, it came to pass that he besieged Ardea, the town of the Rutuli, in Latium; and one evening, when the king's sons were supping with their cousin Tarquinius Collatinus, who lived in Collatia, they talked of their wives, and each praised the virtue and thriftiness of his own wife. Thereupon they agreed to go and see which of the ladies deserved the highest praise. Without delay they mounted their horses and galloped quickly to Rome, and then to Collatia, to take the ladies by surprise. They found the daughters-in-law of the king enjoying themselves at a feast; but Lucretia, the wife of Collatinus, they found sitting up late at night with her maids busy with household work. Therefore Lucretia was acknowledged to be the matron most worthy of praise.

Sextus' outrage on Lucretia.

But Sextus Tarquinius, when he had seen Lucretia,

conceived a base design and came again one evening alone to Collatia. Having been kindly received and led to his chamber, he rose in the middle of the night, when everyone was asleep in the house, and came into Lucretia's chamber and surprised her alone. And when she refused to yield herself to him, he threatened to slay her and to put a murdered slave to lie beside her, and then to tell her husband that he had found her in adultery. Then Lucretia resisted no longer; and the next morning Sextus went away and returned to the camp before Ardea.

But Lucretia sent messengers to Rome and to Ardea to fetch her father Lucretius and her husband Collatinus. These two hastened to Collatia, and with them came Junius Brutus and the noble Publius Valerius Poplicola, and they found Lucretia in her room clothed in mourning. When they were all collected together, Lucretia told them of the deed of Sextus, and of the shame brought upon her, and she made the men swear that they would avenge her. And when she had ended her words she drew a knife and plunged it into her heart and died.

Then the men were overwhelmed with grief, and they carried her corpse to the market-place, and told the people what had happened and sent messengers with the news to the army before Ardea. But Brutus assembled the people together, and spoke to them, and called upon them to resist the tyrant. And the people determined to expel King Tarquinius and his whole house, to abolish the regal power, and to suffer no king any more in Rome. In the place of a king they chose two men who should rule for one year, and should be called not kings but consuls; and for the management of the sacrifices which the king had to offer, they chose a priest, who should be called the king of sacrifices, but should have

Expulsion of the king and establishment of the republic.

no power in the state, and should be subject to the high pontiff. Otherwise they altered nothing in the laws and ordinances of the state, but they let them all remain as they had been during the time of the kings. For the first consuls they chose Lucius Junius Brutus, and Lucius Tarquinius Collatinus. Then they shut the gates against Tarquinius, and the Roman army before Ardea abandoned the hated king and went back to Rome. Thus the death of Lucretia was avenged, and Rome became a free city after it had been subject to kings for two hundred and forty years.

But the wicked Tarquin did not give up all hope of regaining his power. He had still a strong party in Rome, *Conspiracy for the restoration of the king.* especially among the younger patricians. Therefore he sent messengers to Rome on the plea of asking the people to give up his movable property. But the messengers secretly consulted with his adherents how the king could be brought back to Rome. Now one day, when the conspirators were conferring privately together, they were overheard by a slave, who betrayed them to the consuls. Wherefore they were all seized and thrown into prison. But the slave was rewarded with freedom and the Roman citizenship.

Then Brutus, who was consul with Tarquinius Collatinus, showed how a true Roman must love his country more than his own blood. *The patriotism of Brutus* For when it was found that his two sons were among those who wished to bring Tarquin and his family back to Rome, he condemned them to death as traitors, even as he condemned the other conspirators, and did not ask mercy for them of the people, but had the youths bound to the stake before his eyes, and gave orders to the lictor to scourge them and to cut off their heads with the axe. The people were now still more embittered against the banished

Tarquins, and the senate declined to give up their goods, and divided them among the people. But the field between the town and the Tiber, which belonged to the Tarquins and was sown with corn, they consecrated to the god Mars, and called it the field of Mars, and the corn they caused to be cut and thrown into the Tiber. It drifted down the bed of the river to a shallow place, where it became fixed; and as, in the course of time, mud and earth collected there, an island was formed in the river, which was afterwards surrounded by embankments and walls, so that large buildings and temples could be erected on it.

Now after the conspiracy had been discovered and punished, the senate and the people made a law that all who were of the Tarquinian race should be banished for ever; and all the secret adherents of the royal party left the town, and joined the expelled king. *Banishment of the house of the Tarquinii.* But Tarquinius Collatinus, who was consul with Brutus, was a friend of the people and an enemy of the tyrant and his house, on account of the shame which Sextus Tarquinius had brought upon Lucretia his wife. But as he was of the race of the Tarquins, he obeyed the law, laid down his office, and went into exile, and the people chose Publius Valerius to be consul in his place.

Now when the plan of Tarquinius to regain his dominion by cunning and fraud had been defeated, he went to the town of Tarquinii in the land of the Etruscans, which was the home of his father, and he moved the people of Tarquinii and of Veii to make war upon Rome. *War with Tarquinii and Veii.* Then the Romans marched out against the Etruscans, and fought with them near the wood Arsia. And in the battle Aruns, the son of Tarquinius, saw Brutus at the head of the Roman army, and thinking to revenge himself upon the enemy of his house, he put spurs to his horse, and ran against him with his spear. When Brutus saw him, he did the same, and each pierced the other through the body with his spear, so that both fell down dead from their horses. But the battle was fierce and bloody, and lasted until the evening without being decided. And in the night, when both armies were encamped on the field of battle, the voice of the god Silvanus was heard coming out of the wood, saying that the Romans had conquered, for among the Etruscans one man more was slain than among the Romans. Then the Etruscans went away to their homes, and the Romans also marched home, taking the body of Brutus with them, and the Roman matrons mourned for him a whole year, because he had so bravely avenged the wrongs of Lucretia.

Thereupon Tarquin the tyrant betook himself to Clusium, to King Porsenna, who ruled over all the Etruscans, and he implored help of him against the Romans. Then Porsenna collected a powerful army, and marched against Rome to restore Tarquin to his kingdom. And coming on suddenly he took the hill Janiculus, which lies on the right side of the Tiber, opposite the Capitol, and drove the Romans down the hill toward the river. Then the Romans were seized with great fear, and did not venture to oppose the enemy, and to defend the entrance of the bridge, but they fled across the bridge back into the city. When Horatius, who was surnamed Cocles, or the 'one-eyed,' saw this, he placed himself opposite to the enemy, at the entrance of the bridge, while two warriors, who were called Lartius and Herminius, stayed by his side. These three men stirred not from the place, but fought alone with the whole army of the Etruscans, and held their post, while the Romans broke down the bridge behind them. And when only a

War with Porsenna of Clusium.

Horatius Cocles.

few planks were left, Lartius and Herminius hurried back, but Horatius would not move until the whole was broken down and fell into the river. Then he turned round, and with his arms upon him just as he was, sprang into the Tiber and swam back unhurt. Thus Horatius saved Rome from the Etruscans; and the Romans rejoiced and led him in triumph into the city, and afterwards they erected a monument to him on the Comitium, and gave him as much land as he could plough in one day.

Meanwhile, the town was hard pressed by Porsenna, and there arose a famine in Rome, and the people were driven to despair. Then Mucius, a noble Roman, determined to kill King Porsenna, and he went into the Etruscan camp, even into the king's tent. But, as he did not know the king, he slew the treasurer, who sat near him, distributing the pay to the soldiers. And he was seized and threatened with death. Then to show that he was not afraid of death he stretched out his right hand into the fire which was burning on an altar, and kept it in the flame without flinching, until it was burnt to ashes. But Porsenna, when he saw it, was amazed at the firmness of the youth and forgave him, and allowed him to return to his home. To show his gratitude for the magnanimity of Porsenna, Mucius revealed to him that three hundred Roman youths had sworn to attempt the same deed that he had undertaken, and that they would not rest until they had taken his life.

Mucius Scaevola.

When Porsenna heard this, he feared to distress the Romans any longer, and made peace with them. He took no land from them, except seven villages of the Veientines, which the Romans had conquered in former times; and, having received hostages, he insisted no longer that they should receive Tarquin again as their king.

Among the hostages was a noble virgin called Cloelia, who would not suffer herself to be kept captive among the Etruscans. Therefore when the night came, she slipped out of the camp, reached the river, and swam across to Rome. But the Romans, although they honoured her courage, blamed her conduct, and brought her back to Porsenna, because she had acted in opposition to the treaty they had sworn. Then Porsenna admired the faith of the Romans, and released Cloelia and as many of the other hostages as she selected; and when he went away from Rome, he left his camp there and gave to the Romans all the things contained in it.

Cloelia.

When Porsenna had become tired of the war, he went home to Clusium; but he sent his son Aruns, with an army against Aricia, a chief town of the Latins, where the people of Latium were accustomed to meet for council. But Aristodemus, the Greek tyrant of Cumae, helped the Latins, and the Etruscans were beaten in a great battle, so that few escaped alive. These the Romans received hospitably, nursing them and healing their wounds; and to those who wished to remain in Rome they gave dwellings in that part of the town which after them was called the Etruscan quarter.

The Etruscans defeated at Aricia.

But Tarquin had not given up all hopes of regaining his kingdom. Therefore he went to Tusculum, to his son-in-law, Octavius Mamilius, and persuaded the Tusculans and the other Latins to make war upon Rome. And the Romans trembled before the strength of the Latins, and not trusting in the divided command of the two consuls, they nominated a dictator, who should have power over Rome like a king, and be sole leader of the army for six months. For this purpose they chose Marcus Valerius. After this

Latin war.

a great battle was fought between the Romans and the Latins near the Lake Regillus, and the Romans began to give way when the banished king, at the head of a band of Roman exiles, came against them. Then the Roman dictator vowed a temple to Castor and Pollux if they would assist the Romans in battle. And suddenly two youths rode on white chargers at the head of the Roman horse and pressed down upon the enemy. And the Romans saw that they were the sacred twins, and taking courage they overthrew the Latins, and killed many of them. Now, when the battle was lost, Tarquin gave up all hope of regaining his kingdom, and he went to Cumae to the tyrant Aristodemus, and dwelt there till he died.

Battle of Lake Regillus.

CHAPTER IV.

EXAMINATION OF THE LEGENDS OF THE KINGS.

FROM what has been said before, it is clear that the story of the Roman kings is not based even indirectly upon contemporary records of any kind. The only claim which it can possibly make upon our acceptance is that some portions of it embody a faint national tradition preserved for many generations without the aid of writing. What these portions are we have no external criteria to indicate. We must therefore examine the substance of the traditions in the hope that we may succeed in extricating a residuum of truth hidden under a vast superincumbent mass of fiction.

Absence of contemporary records.

The most easily accomplished task is the rejection of

all that is absolutely fabulous. Herein the credulous annalists themselves have preceded us. Even they could not make up their minds to believe in the miraculous conception of the twins and in the equally miraculous suckling she-wolf. They tried to explain away these miracles in a rationalistic way, by suggesting that some lover of Rhea Silvia assumed the form of Mars, and that a woman belonging to the disreputable class vulgarly known as she-wolves (*lupae*) acted as the nurse of the infant twins. This mode of explaining away miracles has lost all favour with modern critics. It is evident that the miracle in the story is not a casual, external ornament, which can be cast aside, but that it is the very germ and centre of the story, the most important and essential part of it, and that without it the narrative is nothing but an empty shell.

<small>Rationalists' explanation of fables.</small>

It is therefore absolutely impossible to save the old miracles of the birth and preservation of Romulus and his brother. In a like manner his ascension into heaven must be sacrificed, though that also was at one time sagaciously supposed to be the poetical version of a very plausible event, viz., his murder by his enemies during the sudden darkness of a thunderstorm. The fact that his body could not be found after the storm was easily accounted for. The senators, who murdered him, cut it up and carried the pieces away under their togas!

We need not rehearse the vain conceits with which the other miracles were turned into plausible history. They are all equally futile, and we have no alternative left but to draw our pen through the whole of them, though thereby we reduce the substance of the so-called history of the kings very considerably and deprive it of those parts which make it most lively and attractive.

But not only the stories which offend against physical laws must be expunged; we must, in the interest of truth, be equally merciless where the stories are incompatible with moral laws. For the world of human feelings and actions is governed by laws as constant as the laws of outward nature, though they are more subtle in their working, and less clear to our comprehension. The statement that during the forty-three years of Numa's reign Rome enjoyed uninterrupted peace cannot be looked upon as anything but a fiction or a dream. No waking and sober mind could imagine that the turbulent Romans and their neighbours, who, in the time of Romulus which preceded and in the time of Tullus Hostilius which followed, hardly sheathed their swords, would out of respect for a pious and peaceful king sit down quietly to work and pray for forty-three years. The peace of Numa's reign is a miracle not less startling than his intercourse with the nymph Egeria or his trick of intoxicating the god Faunus by pouring wine into the fountain of which he drank. *[Moral impossibilities.]*

Objections hardly less weighty than those just mentioned have been raised against the truthfulness of the stories of the kings on the score of chronology. The period assigned to the seven kings embraces two hundred and forty years, which is an average of thirty-four years for each king. Considering that four of the seven kings died by violence, and that one was expelled fifteen years before his death, it is not possible that such a long period should be covered by the reigns of seven elective monarchs. The first to draw attention to this circumstance was Sir Isaac Newton, and now there is no difference of opinion on the point. It suffices to compare the average duration of the reigns of the doges of Venice, who were, like the Roman kings, elective princes. In five centuries (from 805 to 1311 A.D.) forty doges occupied the ducal chair. This gives an average of twelve years and a half to each, or not much *[Chronological impossibilities.]*

more than one-third of the duration assigned to a Roman king. The Roman figures therefore may safely be pronounced to be contrary to the laws of nature. Difficulties of a like kind arise when we scrutinise the data which refer to the lives and reigns of the two Tarquinii. The elder of them is said to have left his native town because it offered him no scope for his ambition. He must therefore have been a man at least approaching middle age. He was then married, and removed with his wife Tanaquil to Rome. Here he lived sixteen years under Ancus Martius. His own reign lasted thirty-eight years. He was then murdered at the instigation of the sons of Ancus, who, by the bye, had waited patiently these thirty-eight years before they tried to recover their father's inheritance. Tarquinius must have been upwards of eighty years old when he died, and his wife more than seventy. Yet their children are represented as of tender age. If we assume that the eldest of them was ten years old on the death of his father, he had reached the age of fifty-four when he rose against Servius Tullius and hurled him down the steps of the senate-house, acting like a man in the first vigour of youth and heat of passion. But if the story, inconsistent with itself, represents the children of the elder Tarquin as sufficiently grown up at the beginning of the reign of Servius to enable the latter to marry them with his own children, the subsequent events become still more incredible. Tarquin the second must, then, have approached the venerable age of seventy when he rose against his father-in-law, must have been more than ninety when he besieged Ardea, and a hundred and eight or ten when he fought in the battle of Lake Regillus.

These are reflexions which do not disturb the poet or the narrator of legends. But the historian is bound to have an eye to the computation of years. Consequently the inherent improbabilities of the story roused the suspicion even of some ancient annalists, and Piso bethought himself of a means of remedying the fault. He inserted a whole generation between the elder and the younger Tarquin, and made the latter the grandson instead of the son of the former. This ingenious little trick of legerdemain met with the approbation of Dionysius. But Livy more honestly tells the story in the old unadulterated form, leaving to his readers the task of reconciling it with the laws of nature.

The objections which we have raised hitherto to the credibility of the ancient story are so obvious and palpable that they have presented themselves even to minds endowed with a very moderate amount of critical acumen, and in ages long preceding the birth of historical criticism. Yet there are other objections in reserve, perhaps less patent at the first glance, but not less destructive of our faith in the traditional story. *Other objections.*

The narrative proceeds on the assumption that the Roman people was formed by Romulus into a distinct national body out of heterogeneous and, as it were, atomic elements. The individuals who compose it flock together from different quarters, and are moulded into a political society by the will of an omnipotent lawgiver. They had no laws before. The organization of the state, the laws which regulate private and public life, were all the creation of Romulus. In like manner the first settlers had hardly a national religion. It was Numa who told them how to pray and worship, who appointed priests, sacrifices, and all that belongs to a public worship. The presumption upon which these accounts rest is altogether erroneous. The study of a great variety of nations has shown us that people who live together in any sort of community might just as well be supposed to be without a *Omnipotent lawgivers.*

common language as without common political institutions and without religious notions and worship.

<small>Laws and religion as primeval as language.</small> None of these essential conditions for the existence of man can be said to have been at any time artificially made for them by any prophet or lawgiver. The utmost that legislators can effect is to modify, to improve, to purify existing systems and institutions. To none of them, that we know of in history, was it given to find a void which he could fill with a theory of his own invention. Laws are not made, but grow. Even now, in our time of restless and over-prolific parliamentary law-making, new laws mark only the endeavours of legislators to find the forms in which the general feeling of justice is to be expressed, or in which new wants, felt by the community, are to be satisfied under public authority.

If we approach the history of the kings with such convictions, we shall at once see that it cannot lay the least claim to authenticity. With the aid of two new sciences, comparative mythology and comparative philology, we can trace back the religion and the social institutions of Rome to an age which preceded the separation of the Latin race from the Sabine; nay, further back than that, to the period when the forefathers of Italians and Greeks, and of all the nations of the Aryan stock, dwelt together and were bound together by unity of language, religion, and social institutions. The received story breaks down in the very attempt to carry out the principle upon which it proceeds. It wishes to represent Numa as the founder of the Roman religion; but it makes Romulus the son of a national god and of a priestess of Vesta, a goddess whose worship was as original and essential as the domestic hearth is for the establishment of a house. All the stories, therefore, referring to the origin of Roman institutions, which, whether religious, political, or social, are anterior to contemporary history or genuine tradition, must be looked upon as fabrications of a later age as endeavours to divine the mysterious process by which law and religion spring into existence. A great portion of the matter that fills up the early history is entirely made up of such endeavours. They take the form of myths, and have been properly called 'aetiological myths,' *i.e.*, myths accounting for causes. Wherever an old ceremony, **rite, or** custom presented itself which seemed to be susceptible of an explanation, a story was invented which satisfied a credulous age as to its origin and meaning. *Aetiological myths.*

To give an illustration of such aetiological myths, we will glance at the story of the rape of the Sabines.

It was a custom at Roman nuptials for the **bride-groom** to pretend to carry off the bride by force from her parents' home. A similar custom is found in Greece, and no doubt prevailed very largely, if not universally, in antiquity, as traces of it can be discovered even now in many **parts of** Europe. To what extent this simulated violence **was the** remnant and reflex of real violence used in still **earlier ages,** we need not now inquire. It suffices to **know that the** custom existed. This custom seemed to require an historical explanation. How and when, people asked, did it originate? An answer was found in the story of the rape of the Sabines. It was said that the custom originated in the violence committed by Romulus, whereas the **relation** of cause and effect is the very **reverse.** The story originated in the custom, not the custom from the story, and this is, therefore, not a genuine tradition of a real event, but a fiction pure and simple or an aetiological myth. *The rape of the Sabines.*

Such fictions were at first shamefaced and modest. At least they did not pretend to historical **truth.** Therefore the number of the Sabine women carried off by the Romans was stated to have been thirty, that is to say, as many as there were curies at Rome. In this form it was, on the very face of it, a fable intended to please and to amuse. But by-and-by such fables were worked up into historical statements. It was plain that the number of thirty was too small. What were thirty women among so many men? Consequently some ingenious annalists gravely asserted that the number of the Sabines, all counted, was exactly five hundred and twenty-seven. Who could now doubt the accuracy of the report? It was evident that the number must have been taken from a memorandum entered by Romulus himself, or at least by the first Pontifex Maximus, in the public archives!

Not only laws and customs but also the names and the characteristics of localities supplied the materials for aetiological myths. In the Roman Forum there was a spot called Lacus Curtius, marked by a peculiar pavement or an enclosure. According to a statement preserved by Varro, this spot was struck by lightning in the year 445 B.C., and Curtius, one of the consuls of the year, inclosed it, by order of the senate. This is in all probability the true account. But it was either forgotten or it did not satisfy the popular fancy. Accordingly a more striking story was invented. Once upon a time the earth opened in the Forum and no efforts would avail to close it. Then the soothsayers declared that the gods of death demanded the life of the bravest citizen, whereupon Curtius mounted his charger and fully armed leapt down into the gulf, which instantly closed upon him. Hence the spot where the chasm had been was called the Curtian Lake. Here was an evident miracle. But some rational annalist who was above the faith in childish miracles wanted sober, sensible facts, which could be given out as historical. So he set to

The Lacus Curtius.

work and related how that in the war between Romulus and Titus Tatius a certain Sabine horseman named Curtius, charging the Romans, plunged into and was with difficulty extricated from a swamp in the valley between the two hills where afterwards the Forum was laid out. After this Sabine warrior the spot was named for ever afterwards the Lake of Curtius.

It would be useless to enumerate and discuss all the aetiological myths of which the history of the kings is full. They all bear the same character, and are easily stripped of their deceitful historical mask and exhibited in their own fabulous hollowness.

Some of the liveliest and most attractive portions of the early annals of Rome are stories of Greek origin smuggled in at a time when Greek slaves and Greek poets began to flatter their Roman patrons, stories. either by trying to connect the early history of the two nations, or by adorning the dry and barren waste of the Roman annals with flowers culled in the luxurious gardens of their own imagination.

These Greek stories are easily detected, not only from their intrinsic character, but because we can sometimes point out the very spot in the literature of Greece from which they are taken. The story of the Tarquinii especially is enlivened by such contributions from Greek fiction. The stratagem by which Sextus, the son of Tarquin, gained the confidence of the people of Gabii is copied from Herodotus, who relates it of Zopyrus and Darius. The dumb message sent by Tarquin to his son at Gabii, giving him to understand that he should cut off the heads of the foremost men, is identical with one which, according to the same author, was sent by Thrasybulus, the tyrant of Miletus, to his friend Periander of Corinth. The embassy to the Delphian oracle is another instance of Greek fiction mixed up with Roman annals; for how should the Romans have consulted Greek oracles more than two hundred years before even the name of Rome was heard in Greece?

But a legend far more intimately connected with the most essential part of Roman story than the anecdotes just referred to, is no doubt an importation from Greece, viz., the legend of the miraculous birth and preservation of Romulus and Remus.

The legend of Romulus not of Roman origin.

We have already had an opportunity of remarking that the deities of the Roman Pantheon were not invested like those of the Greeks with human forms and attributes. At least it may be affirmed that the faculty of personifying their gods was possessed by the Romans only in a rudimentary condition. They looked upon the gods as either male or female, it is true; but there is no trace of a Roman theogony, of a Roman Olympus where the gods lived in the fashion of men, marrying and begetting children. All the myths, therefore, which tell of the loves of the gods in a human form may be suspected of being borrowed from Greece. Hence the apparition of Mars, in full armour, to the affrighted Vestal, and his becoming the father of Romulus and Remus, are features which betray the Greek origin of the legend. The wonderful preservation of the exposed children, especially the suckling by the she-wolf, are features clearly taken from similar myths, which appear to have been numerous in Greece and the East, and of which that of the infant Cyrus (afterwards King of Persia) is a type. From the same source sprung the story of the apotheosis of Romulus; for though the Romans worshipped the spirits of the departed as divine beings, able to bless or to hurt the living, yet they were ignorant of the genuine hero-worship which filled the Greek cities with shrines and sepulchres of local deities supposed to be sprung from a mortal race.

Whatever we may think of the origin of these myths, whether they are, as we suppose, imported from Greece or whether they grew on Italian soil, nobody will deny that they are myths, or pretend that they contain even a residuum of genuine historical traditions.

We now come to another force which has been active in the formation of the **legendary history** of the Roman kings, and which is due to that poverty of imagination characteristic of the Roman people, to which we have already referred. Meagreness of Roman imagination. Not endowed with a fancy fertile enough to invent stories sufficient to fill the period of two hundred and forty years, the Roman pontiffs, or whoever drew up the first systematic plan of the earliest history, multiplied events by varying the detail of the same original story, and relating the different versions successively. It is possible that before the first attempt at a systematic arrangement of the details which make up the history of the kings, these details were separately current as conceptions which different people had formed, independently of one another, about the primeval period. The compilers thereupon made use of as much as suited their purpose, adjusting and fitting the materials so as to form a plausible story, consistent in itself and free from palpable contradictions. But their success was not great. As shown above, they could not even assign the proper place to the political and to the religious lawgiver. In their endeavour to attribute to each of the kings some peculiar policy which might fill his reign, they were driven to represent a whole generation of Romans as destitute of the fundamental religious institutions. Other defects in the story may easily be discovered. Those which refer to the chronology have been already pointed out; but the repetition of the same facts under a slight disguise of different names and circumstances is perhaps the most Repetitions.

decisive proof of the flimsiness of that web which is so fair to look at, but which falls to pieces as soon as it is touched by the hand of criticism.

We will give a few specimens. It cannot have escaped the most careless reader that there is a great resemblance between Romulus and Tullus Hostilius. They are both warlike; both double the number of Roman citizens, the one by union with the Sabines, the other by the reduction of Alba. The war with Alba, again, has its prototype in the war with Titus Tatius. As Tullus Hostilius is opposed to Mettius Fufetius, so under Romulus Hostus Hostilius fights with Mettius Curtius; the two Hostilii and Mettii are so clearly identical that the addition of second names, which is intended to disguise the identity, cannot deceive us. Besides, Tullus as well as Romulus has grown up among shepherds; both join Mount Caelius to the city, both organise the Roman army, both introduce the insignia of regal power, the 'sella curulis,' or chair of state, the lictors, and the embroidered toga, both degenerate into tyrants, and finally both are removed from earth amidst thunder and lightning and are seen no more.

<small>Identity of Romulus and Tullus;</small>

The similarity thus apparent between Romulus and Tullus Hostilius has its counterpart in the stories of Numa and Ancus. The latter is evidently the shadow of the former. Both are essentially priests; the former nominates a high pontiff, Numa Marcius, to whom he confides the sacred books. Evidently this Numa Marcius, who combines the names of the two kings, is a creature of the same fiction which represented the founder of the Roman worship as a sacerdotal king. As Numa's reign had been emphatically peaceful, he could not be made to establish the religious ceremonies to be observed in declaring war. Consequently this task was given to Ancus, and a war with the Latins was ascribed to him, which helped to make the stories of the

<small>of Numa and Ancus:</small>

two kings look different. Nevertheless the original identity of Numa and Ancus is sufficiently apparent. Both are 'bridgemakers.' Numa is 'pontifex' (as it was supposed, from *pons*, bridge, and *facere*, to make, although the word denoted properly the priestly leader of a procession), and to Ancus is ascribed the construction of the wooden bridge over the Tiber. Finally, the two are the only kings who die a natural and peaceful death.

The original identity of the first and second Tarquin need hardly be demonstrated. But there are sufficient indications to show that they were also looked upon as the political and military lawgivers of Rome, in fact that they are identical with Romulus and Tullus. Servius Tullius combines in himself the character of the two classes of Roman kings, who alternate in the annalistic scheme of the primeval period. He is the author of social and peaceful order, and of civil law like Numa, and he also introduces a military organization which makes him identical with Romulus. According to a casually preserved tradition, his birth was as miraculous as that of the founder of the city. His mother was a vestal virgin and his father a god, who appeared to her on the hearth, the domestic altar, of which she had the charge. By this birth he is really characterised as the founder of the city, for it appears from other similar legends that Italian cities ascribed their origin as a rule to sons of Vestals and the gods of the hearth. *of the two Tarquins, Romulus and Tullus; of Servius Tullius.*

It is generally supposed that the latter portion of the legendary history of Rome has a more historical character than the earlier. Scholars who are prepared to give up Romulus and Numa as fabulous beings, and who look upon Tullus and Ancus as prehistoric, would fain persuade themselves that the stories of Servius Tullius and the Tarquins contain a great deal of genuine historical *The latter part of the history of the kings as fabulous as the first.*

truth. Unfortunately this is an assumption which upon examination appears to be unfounded. If, on the whole, the family history of the Tarquinian dynasty has not so mythical a character as that of the preceding kings, it is perhaps even more full of arbitrary fiction and untrustworthy statements. We have referred already to the chronological absurdities which pervade it, and to the stories of foreign growth with which it is decked out. Nor is the supernatural element wanting. Not to speak of the miraculous birth of Servius, and the light which blazed round the head of the sleeping child, we see that the prophetic queen Tanaquil, the arrival in Rome of the weird Sibylla, and the stories of prodigies with which the narrative is interwoven, are not of a character to give us more confidence. So much for the bona-fide miracles. Let us see if the story shows more respect for the canons of historical probability than for physical laws.

King Servius is represented as the author of the scheme which divided the people into five classes according to a property qualification, and into 194 centuries, as the subdivision of the classes. This is the celebrated constitution of centuries, the groundwork of the centuriate comitia of the people, which, constantly adapted to the changing condition of the times, lasted to the end of the republic. Now, we are asked to believe, on the strength of the fabulous story of the kings, that Servius, having drawn up this elaborate scheme, was prevented by his sudden death (though he is reported to have reigned forty-four years) from actually bringing it into operation, that it remained a dead letter during the whole reign of Tarquin the younger, and that upon his expulsion Brutus availed himself of this ready-made constitution to establish the republic upon it. Although the people had never yet been called upon to meet in

The miraculous origin of the Servian constitution.

the centuriate assemblies for electoral or legislative purposes, they fell in so readily with the political ideas of Servius, that forthwith centuriate comitia could be held, the monarchy abolished by a vote of the people thus assembled, and the new republican order started in all its completeness, with two annual and responsible consuls instead of a king for life, and with all the modifications of the old laws consequent upon the change.

It need hardly be said that such a process is all but miraculous. History shows that constitutional changes which have any life in them and are destined to last are not concocted in the closet of a lawgiver, nor put into working order without much difficulty and opposition. The ease and facility with which Tarquinius is deposed at Rome, and the republic established without bloodshed, resembles a genuine revolution as much as a military review or a sham fight resembles a genuine battle. *Expulsion of Tarquinius equally miraculous.* How can we suppose that a powerful king like Tarquinius, without having suffered so far any check either at home or in foreign war, a king who is represented as acknowledged lord of Latium, and who after a time marshals all Latium against Rome, should be thus cast out of his kingdom, not in consequence of a long-prepared conspiracy, and a powerful and organized opposition, but by a sudden and unexpected explosion of popular passion, caused by an outrage, committed not by the king himself, but by one of his sons? And to enter into the detail of this alleged outrage, what can be more absurd than the dispute in the camp among the young princes concerning the domestic virtues of their wives, the night ride to Rome and Collatia, and all that follows? How, for instance, can it be supposed that Sextus did not know his cousin's wife, until he saw her working late among her servants on this occasion? Lucretia's death may be a good subject for the epic or dramatic poet, but in the pages of sober history it is an idle tale.

The foreign history of this period is not a whit more plausible or credible. We will select two portions—the war with Porsenna and the Latin war—to show that our doubts are fully justified. If we succeed in this, it will hardly be necessary to subject the remainder of the story to a similar examination, for it will not be supposed likely that the earlier portions of the narrative deserve more credit than the later.

Incredibility of the foreign history.

The war with Porsenna is among those parts of early Roman history which first attracted and justified the scepticism of modern scholars. And, in truth, the narrative in itself is so absurd and contradictory, that even without any external testimony we may safely pronounce the events to be unreal. Porsenna is represented as a great king of Etruria, who undertakes a war for the purpose of restoring Tarquin to his throne. He drives the Romans into their city, lays siege to it, and compels the people by famine to sue for peace, and actually to give hostages. Nevertheless at the conclusion of peace no mention is made of the object for which the war was undertaken. Tarquinius is not brought back to Rome. Porsenna disappears from the stage, proving in the end not an enemy but a benefactor of the Romans, restoring the hostages, leaving the Romans his camp for public use, and giving them back the land on the right bank of the Tiber of which he had intended to deprive them.

The war of Porsenna resulted in the subjugation of Rome.

So much of contradiction is contained in the narrative of Livy. But this narrative seems coloured in the interest of Roman vanity. Pliny has preserved a statement that Porsenna in the treaty of peace forbade the Romans to use iron for any other purpose than agriculture.

This statement, so humiliating to Roman pride, would not have been made if the fact of the subjugation of Rome by an Etruscan king had not been incontestable. The supremacy of this Etruscan king was according to Dionysius formally acknowledged by the Romans, inasmuch as they sent him the insignia of royalty, a sceptre, a purple robe, and an ivory chair. It seems clear, therefore, that a war so successful could not have been a resultless episode of the struggle which the Romans had to make to maintain their independence The war of Porsenna, as it is described in the annals, if it be not a mere fiction, must belong to a different period.

As for the detail with which the account of the war is filled, it is, if not miraculous, at least a poetical ornament, admirably suited for such lays as Macaulay has given us of ancient Rome, but not for a Roman history. The stout Horatius 'who kept the bridge so well in the brave days of old' is a hero like the Homeric Ajax fighting with a host of Trojans to defend the Grecian ships. He reminds us suspiciously of the other Horatius who fought as the champion of Rome in the time of King Tullus. The story of the undaunted Mucius Scævola, who burnt his right hand and thus became left-handed, is apparently nothing but an attempt to explain the origin of the name of Scævola, which means 'left,' and which was a surname of a branch of the Mucian house. Nor is it a very plausible fiction: the Etruscan king seeing his soldiers receive their pay, the paymaster looking like the king, the Roman edging his way into the royal tent and after all striking the wrong man, the king lost in admiration of the stout-hearted Roman, and at the same time so terrified that he grants peace to the enemies whom he had conquered,—all these are features of a story too childish to be tolerated in history.

The war of Porsenna must, therefore, be struck out of

the annals which purpose to recount the establishment of the Republic.

The Latin war which terminated with the battle of Lake Regillus is of a different character. It seems to be real and to have taken place about the time assigned to it; but its aim and object are entirely misstated and the detail is fictitious. We will endeavour to prove the first part of this assertion lower down, when we review the historical residuum of the fables and traditions of this period. Here we will only direct attention to the perversion of truth and to the arbitrary fiction apparent in the vulgar narrative.

The Latin war full of fictions.

The description given of the battle of Lake Regillus is altogether poetical, and seems almost copied from Homer. The leaders engage in single combat and perform feats of personal prowess. It is essentially a cavalry engagement. The infantry, in which we know that the strength of the Roman armies always consisted, goes for nothing. Victory is decided in the end by the charge of the Roman knights headed by the divine twins Castor and Pollux. This feature shows that the poetic colouring of the story is Greek; for the identical legend, of aid given by Castor and Pollux in battle, occurs in the annals of the Greek city of Locri in southern Italy.

The time when the battle of Lake Regillus was fought is variously stated by various authors. It seems strange that, if the battle was so decisive as is generally assumed, its date should be uncertain. But we may entertain grave doubts about its decisiveness, when we find that the Latins, who are reported to have been utterly crushed in it, concluded a league with Rome soon afterwards on a footing of equality.

CHAPTER V.

THE FIVE PHASES OF THE HISTORY OF ROME IN THE REGAL PERIOD.

We have now examined the salient features of the history of the kings, and have come to the conclusion that it is no history at all. Shall we rest here, satisfied with this negative result? Shall we cut off all that precedes the establishment of the republic as mere idle play of the imagination, or is it possible to save something out of the wreck, and to substitute a few great outlines for the elaborate drawing with all the fanciful detail? Can we suppose that, after all, the memory of some events of the earliest period did remain in the popular mind with sufficient distinctness to supply the earliest annalists with an historical substratum for their narrative, or are there, perhaps, in the institutions of the republic certain features from which we may infer what sort of institutions preceded them? We think we may safely proceed upon the former as well as upon the latter hypothesis, and assert that by disclaiming the intention of giving a consecutive narrative, by passing over most of the names and dates with which we have been teased so long, we shall be able to draw a picture—necessarily imperfect, but historically true—of the political condition of the Roman people in the earliest period, and of the national and political revolutions through which it passed.

There is every reason for believing that long before Rome became powerful, the whole of Latium was filled with a number of independent city-communities. In fact, this is the assumption upon which the Roman tradition itself proceeds. It is quite credible also, that these Latin cities had esta- *[Most ancient state of Latium.]*

A. H.

blished a sort of confederacy, and that at the head of this confederacy was Alba Longa. In historical times Alba Longa lay in ruins. Nevertheless the people of Latium annually assembled near its site, where the temple of Jupiter Latiaris had been left standing, and there they celebrated the Latin games (*feriae Latinae*) and offered a joint sacrifice to Jupiter as a sign and memorial of their being all members of a national confederation. Rome had then the presidency at these meetings, occupying the place which originally no doubt belonged to Alba Longa. It is not likely that such a custom would have been introduced after the fall of Alba, whereas we can easily understand that if established at the time of Alban preponderance, it was continued in the same spot ever after in that spirit of conservatism which is natural to all religions, but was especially characteristic of the religion of Rome.

A confederacy under Alba as head.

We may suppose that, in this period of the power of Alba, the hills of Rome were occupied by Latin settlers, like all the sites in Latium, which were capable of being easily converted into strongholds. The Romans of that period, therefore, were Latins, and the Roman language has retained for ever after the name of Latin, testifying thereby the original identity of race.

Rome a Latin settlement.

This, then, is the first phase of Roman history.

The second stage begins with the invasion of Latium by a kindred race, the Sabines. That such an invasion took place at an early period is certain, even if the story of Titus Tatius and the people of Cures, coming down the valley of the Tiber, conquering the Capitoline and the Quirinal hills, and settling in Rome, were not related in the annals, and did not bear the aspect of a genuine tradition. For among the oldest and most permanent institutions of Rome,

Invasion of Latium by Sabines.

among their religious rites and their deities, there are some which are admitted on all sides to be of Sabine origin. It is therefore highly probable that Sabines settled on some of the hills of Rome, as the annals relate, and also that at the same time other Latin cities passed into the hands of the same invaders, for it is not likely that the hills of Rome were the only attraction (as the story of the rape would make us believe), and we do find that actually some of the cities of Latium between the Tiber and the Anio were Sabine in population. Perhaps it was in the course of this Sabine invasion that Alba Longa, the head of Latium, was taken and destroyed.

This is the second phase of the history of Rome.

The annalists have preserved traditions of hostilities between the original Latin settlers on the Palatine and the invaders who held the Capitol and the Quirinal. Such hostilities might safely be assumed to have taken place even if no tradition had preserved the memory of them. As we have seen above (p. 6), nothing is more likely than that the independent communities, living in such proximity to one another, found it more advantageous to come to terms and to live in peace and friendship, than to harass each other in daily strife. Accordingly, they agreed to a kind of international alliance, and in doing so they followed the example of the Latin cities, and, as far as we can see, the custom of all the Italian races, who seem everywhere to have formed confederacies where circumstances favoured or necessitated them. *Alliance of Romans and Sabines.*

This is the third phase of the history of Rome.

The alliance of Romans and Sabines was the condition of the future greatness of Rome; for the strength of the several communities, instead of being worn out by internal strife, was now combined and soon gave Rome a pre-

ponderance over the smaller Latin towns. But the proximity to each other of the members of the Roman confederacy was such, their intercourse so frequent, their interests so nearly identical, that a mere international alliance was soon found an insufficient bond of union, and thus it was deve-
Alliance developed into a federal state. loped into some sort of closer political union, or a federal state. This step is indicated in the tradition of the annalists, when they say that the senate was raised from one hundred to two hundred members, that the number of the citizens was doubled, and that the two kings, Romulus and Tatius, agreed to reign in common. The Roman state had now outgrown the political organization at which the leagues of the Latins, and of the other Italian peoples, stopped. All the other leagues were international, leaving each member free to support or to oppose the policy of the majority. The Romans, starting from the same point, advanced further, and bound up the free will and independence of the members in the national will, declared by the decisions of a common senate and a popular assembly.

This was the fourth phase of the history of Rome.

Rome had now become a federal state, consisting of a union of families, which formed curies and tribes. The head of this community was a king, elected for life, and combining the functions of high priest with those of judge and military chief. But of these three functions the first seems to have been by far the most prominent and important in the earliest period of the monarchy, as will appear more fully lower down. Religion is older than any other element in human society. Political institutions and civil laws are modelled upon religious institutions and divine law, and are a secondary development in the history of nations. Though in the conventional arrangement of the Roman kings, Romulus precedes Numa, the institutions of Numa must be older than those of Romulus; in other words, the oldest kings of Rome were pre-eminently priests, and the oldest constitution was more akin to a federation of half-independent families than to a fully developed state.

How long this kind of priest-kingship lasted we cannot tell. It was followed by a military monarchy, which abolished the old sacerdotal constitution, raised the military and civil power over that of the priestly order, consolidated and strengthened the state, and thus intensified the preponderance of Rome over the other Latin cities. *The sacerdotal king superseded by a military king.*

This is the fifth phase in the history of Rome. It appears in the traditional story as the reigns of the Tarquins and Servius Tullius, and it seems to coincide with the influence of Etruscan dominion over Latium.

The nation of the Etruscans differed widely from the Latins and their kinsmen the Sabines. They spoke a language not understood by their neighbours. They were far advanced in civilisation, in architecture and the other arts, in trade, navigation, and manufactures, when the Romans were still half barbarians. Their settlements stretched at one time from the Alps to Campania. Latium lay between Campania and Etruria proper; it was therefore the country through which the Etruscans had to pass, if they proceeded southwards by land. Nor are traces of Etruscan dominion wanting in Latium. The city of Tusculum betrays by its very name a Tuscan, i.e. an Etruscan, origin; the town of Fidenae, close to Rome, is admitted to have been Etruscan; Mezentius, an old Etruscan king, is said to have ruled in Latium; and the story of Porsenna relates the victory of an Etruscan king over the Romans. Finally, what is perhaps the most significant hint, the insignia of the Roman kings (p. 45) were those of the *The Etruscans.* *Etruscan dominion in Latium.*

kings of Etruria. If, in addition to all these indications, we find that some of the Roman kings were supposed to have come from Etruria, we have no difficulty in arriving at the conclusion that these kings were Etruscan conquerors.

In accordance with this view we find that the Roman tradition ascribes to the elder Tarquin changes in the old institutions of Rome, in which he had to face the opposition of the native priesthood. In the new organization of the army, Tarquinius Priscus is obliged to yield so far to the objections of Attus Navius, the augur, that he adapts his reforms to the old names and divisions. In removing some old Sabine sanctuaries from a site where he wishes to build the great temple of the Etruscan trinity of gods, Jupiter, Juno, and Minerva, he is obliged to respect the shrines of Juventas and Terminus. It is but a link in this chain, that the second king in this line, Servius, gives a secular and military character to the Roman institutions by devising the centuriate assembly, an organization on the basis of property qualifications for the purpose of government and war. This organization effectually did away with the old religious curiatic assemblies, from which all political power was now taken. If we are justified in supposing that simultaneously the old sacerdotal king, the *Rex*, was stripped of his influence, and that the chief priesthood was conferred on the pontiffs, we shall understand in its totality the great change which raised Rome, from an aristocratic confederacy under a sacerdotal head, to a military monarchy, in which the priesthood was subordinate to the state and in which law and policy were no longer ecclesiastical but secular.

Reforms of Tarquin and Servius.

The old aristocracy appears to have been dissatisfied, because the military kings curtailed their influence. The power of the senate was abridged; but the common people were well disposed towards the kings, who were their natural protectors. In the relation of Rome to Latium a change seems to have taken place. If hitherto Rome had been only a member of the Latin confederacy, she now became its head. Nay, the preponderance of Rome under the Etruscan kings seems to have assumed the form of actual dominion. How long this period lasted we have no means of judging. It seems, however, not to have continued long enough to change the national character or to affect the language of the Romans and the Latins. At last a reaction took place. Political opposition seems to have been backed by national animosity. The Etruscan kings were expelled. The Romans and the Latins regained their independence at the same time. A partial but not a total restoration then took place. The old federal and sacerdotal institutions were not revived. The title of sacerdotal king (*Rex sacrificulus* or *Rex sacrorum*) was allowed to continue; but the office remained stripped of all political influence and limited to some insignificant religious formalities. The old comitia of curies were also preserved, but they no longer possessed any power in the state. The sovereignty of the people was lodged in the centuriate comitia, and the executive power in magistrates who were not chosen for life and consequently invested with irresponsible power, but whose tenure of office was limited to the space of one year. To this limitation was added another. Two men were elected to fill the chief office as colleagues, so that each might be a check on the other, if he acted unlawfully. Otherwise the prerogatives of the Royal office, as exercised by the late kings, were not curtailed.

Thus the period of the military monarchy, though it was not destined to last for ever, and though it did not last

Effect of the military monarchy.

The revolution.

The republic.

perhaps for many generations, was the means of developing out of the old sacerdotal institutions under a priest-king that military organization which was equal to the task of making Rome the mistress of Italy and of the world.

With the republic began the sixth phase in the history of Rome.

CHAPTER VI.

RELIGIOUS INSTITUTIONS IN THE TIME OF THE KINGS.

GIVING up all details of the traditional history of the kings, we have tried to discover through the haze of fiction a few prominent land-marks, by which we have traced the probable course of events from the time when the first settlers arrived on the seven hills of Rome to the establishment of a regular republican government under annually elected magistrates. We will now endeavour to draw a picture of the public life of the Roman people in that primeval period, so that we may have a starting-point, from which to measure the advance made in the succeeding ages, and a background to relieve the life and action of historical times.

Materials for a sketch.
How, it may be asked, shall we obtain the materials for this picture, as the history of the time to which the picture belongs is lost? Shall we not fall into an error as great as that for which we blame the annalists? Shall we not be obliged to draw upon our fancy alone? And will not our picture be as worthless as the legends which we have condemned?

Fortunately it is not so. The advance of historical science since the days of the Roman annalists has enabled us to reproduce pictures of the society even of prehistoric ages, with almost as much objective truth as the geologist can reproduce the fauna and the flora of ages preceding the creation of man and the present conformation of the earth's surface. The heroic period of Greek national life, the age of the Trojan war, and of all that follows down to the Doric migration, is lost to history as much as the period of the Roman kings. Yet it is possible to form a full and accurate conception of life in this period, of the state of society, of government and religion, nay of domestic arrangements, and even of articles of dress and furniture. This we are enabled to do because the epic poetry of Greece, though it cannot be trusted as evidence to prove historical events, invests its ideal personages with real properties, attributes, and qualities, abstracted from what actually came under the poet's observation. If the author of the Odyssey tells of Nausicaa and her troop of maid-servants washing the family linen by the river outside the town, we shall infer not that there ever lived a real princess called Nausicaa, but that in the heroic times the daughters of kings were in the habit of superintending the family washing.

The epic poetry of Greece.

This is well understood nowadays. But the case is somewhat different when we approach the prehistoric period of Rome. Here we have no epic poems, originating in the age we wish to study, and therefore representing the general state of society correctly. The Romans, as we have had occasion to remark, had no national epic poetry. Memory unaided by poetry may preserve striking events of national importance, but will it linger on habits and customs which have passed away? We can hardly think this possible, and we must therefore draw our information concerning the institutions of the regal period from other sources.

Fortunately these are not altogether wanting. We

have already referred to the conservative spirit of the Romans, which induced them to preserve the forms and outward observances of old institutions long after those institutions were practically abolished, and the forms had become empty and unmeaning. Wherever, therefore, we can discover such forms, we are justified in concluding that they had once possessed life and vigour, and from the totality of such isolated fragments we can reconstruct the outlines of the old social and political life.

Conservative spirit of the Romans.

We start with a fact which we have had occasion to refer to in a previous chapter (p. 68), viz., that religious ideas and institutions are the oldest inheritance of a nation, and that they precede those which are secular and political. The earliest periods in the history of every nation may be called sacerdotal or religious. All human action was then inspired, directed, and judged from a religious point of view; the laws were the laws of God; the people was a community of worshippers; the temple of the national deity was the centre of the state; the priests, as the interpreters of the divine will, ruled and regulated society; the national wealth and the national strength were devoted to uphold this system.

Great antiquity of religious institutions.

The truth of this statement is borne out by what we know of the Oriental nations. The Egyptians, the Jews, the Hindoos based their political institutions upon a religious foundation. The sacred books, which contained the religious laws, were at the same time the code which regulated social and political life. Obligations towards the national religion, its creed and worship, were not distinguished from moral obligations, nor moral obligations from those of civil law. The whole life of those nations was bound up in subjection to one idea, the idea of religion.

Supremacy of religion in the East.

As long as the nations of antiquity preserved independent national existence, every religion was strictly a national religion, every god a national god, whose authority extended no further than the boundaries of the state. The god of one state could not claim worship from the citizens of another; nay, he repudiated such worship as sacrilegious and illegitimate. And in a citizen it would have been treason of the worst kind if he had paid homage to any other than the national gods. Purity of religion was a civic virtue; devotion to the altars of the gods was essential to patriotism. Exclusion from the national worship was equivalent to political banishment. A man who had lost his altar had lost his home. *Every religion purely national.*

This unity or oneness of state and religion impresses on all the ancient communities a more or less hierarchical character, although the nations of the West, both Greeks and Italians, differed widely from those of the East, inasmuch as they never made themselves the slaves of a priestly caste and early emancipated the state from the bondage of laws which claimed to be divine and therefore unchangeable. *Hierarchical character of civil communities.*

Yet the earliest period of the Roman people may emphatically be called religious or rather sacerdotal. The law was in the custody of the pontiffs. The punishment of offences consisted in an offering or payment made to the gods in the form of a fine or ransom (*poena*), or it was a solemn act of supplication addressed to the gods to appease their anger by the punishment (*supplicium*) of the offender. Civil claims were prosecuted by a *sacramentum*, i.e. by depositing a sum in the hands of priests, which the losing party forfeited to the gods. Every political association was placed under the control of a protecting deity: for every action, whether private or public, the consent of *Political institutions originally religious.*

the deity had first to be obtained. The father of every family was a priest; every house (*gens*) or association of families had its sanctuary; so had the *curia*, or association of houses, every quarter of a town, every tribe, and finally the state itself. The temple of Vesta was the symbolic hearth of the whole nation in the old Sabino-Latin town. The temple of Jupiter erected by the Tarquins on the Capitol was the centre of the enlarged state; the temple of Diana on the Aventine united the Romans and their allies, the Latins, as fellow-worshippers and fellow-citizens, as the old temple of Jupiter Latiaris on the Alban mount had anciently united all the members of the Latin confederacy.

The pervading influence of religion in the first formation of society and political institutions is thus sufficiently clear, and it follows that to understand the true character and working of these institutions we must try to understand the nature of that religion.

The religion of the Romans, though belonging to that class of polytheism which prevailed, as far as we can see, among all the branches of the Aryan race, differed widely not only from that of the Asiatic nations, but also from that of the Greeks, their nearest neighbours. It agreed in so far as it was a worship of the powers of nature, both material and spiritual. The heavens, the sun and the moon, light, water, the earth, the powers presiding over generation and destruction, health and sickness, the ruling passions of the human heart, the protectors of law and society, all were singled out from the all-pervading godhead, the life and spirit of the world, to receive separate and special worship from man. While other nations speculated with more or less perseverance on the nature and attributes of the divine beings, and laid down elaborate systems of the birth and genealogy of the gods,

The religion of the Romans.

investing them with human forms and passions, the Romans never indulged in such speculations, but were satisfied to look upon their gods as spiritual beings, all-powerful to hurt or to benefit man; they never worked out a philosophical system of religion; in fact, they had no theology and no sacred books to base it on. Before they became directly or indirectly acquainted with the Greeks, they had at best only a rudimentary mythology, and consequently there are no myths of genuine Roman growth (page 72). It is related that in the beginning of the regal period there were no images of gods, but only symbols, such as a lance or a stone. The representations of the gods in human forms were introduced by the Etruscans, who had borrowed them from the Greeks of the Italian peninsula. Thus began a regular process of naturalisation of the Greek deities; the whole system of Greek theology, *Adoption of the Greek mythology.* their myths and their sacred art, were bodily transplanted to fill the void which the unimaginative and unspeculative character of the Romans, and in fact of all the Italians, had left in their religion. Zeus was identified with Jupiter, Hérê with Juno, Athênê with Minerva, Ares with Mars, although the original conceptions of their nature might have been very different. Some Greek and even some Asiatic deities were adopted into the family of the Roman national gods. In short—as far as the speculative and imaginative part of religion was concerned, that is, the theological system, or the articles of faith, if we might use this expression—the religion of Rome became identified with that of Greece.

But the case was different with respect to that part of religion which springs not from reflexion and fancy, but from feeling. The relation between God and man, the sentiments with which the gods were approached, the duties which they exacted, the worship prescribed for their service, in short the LAW, or the practical as distinguished from the theoretical part, were peculiarly Roman, and remained so even when the whole host of the Greek Olympus had migrated to Rome. What the Romans understood by religion was confined to this second part, as by far the more important; through it alone religion could exercise an influence on real life, private as well as public, and it is this which must therefore engage our special attention.

If the religion of the Greeks was more fully and richly developed than that of the Romans on the side of speculation, the Romans on the other hand cultivated the Law with more zeal and earnestness. In fact, they almost resemble some Oriental nations, Aryan and Semitic, in the scrupulous minuteness into which they bent the most trifling transactions of life under the yoke of religious duties. It is true they were free from the minute regulations concerning eating which in the East were an important and characteristic part of religious Law. They did not know the difference between clean and unclean animals, nor were the eastern laws of fasting and manifold washings imposed upon them. All asceticism was unknown to them. But nevertheless the observances prescribed by their religion were so numerous and imperative that no transaction of any importance was free from them. Prayers, offerings, vows, religious ceremonies, minutely regulated for every emergency, were of vital importance. The least oversight, the least neglect might draw down the anger of the gods. Even ignorance was no excuse, for the divine interpreters of the will of the gods were at hand to expound the law and to prescribe for every occasion the proper rite of worship.

Minute religious observances

On the other hand, in return for faithful service, the devout Roman had a right to expect from his gods help, protection, and all the blessings of life. The gods had made a covenant with him, and they were bound to perform their part of the mutual obligation, if he was scrupulous in performing his own. In fact, the word RELIGION is of the same root as OBLIGATION; and whereas the latter is applied to denote a covenant entered into between one citizen and another according to the rules of civil law, the word religion denotes that bondage or service which man owes to the gods on the understanding that he is entitled to an equivalent. But inasmuch as man is the weaker party in wisdom as well as in power, he must be most attentive to perform minutely his part of the agreement. Religion therefore turns out to be the fear lest the gods should punish men for neglect; it is a constant anxiety about duties they have to perform, a scrupulousness which makes them watch their own actions and all external events, lest the anger of the gods should be roused, and it is often not to be distinguished from superstition. Such a religion would have struck paralysing terror into the hearts of men, and would have rendered them ignoble, crouching slaves, if a protection had not been found in the law itself to shield mortal man from the superior power of the gods.

Meaning of the word 'religion.'

The religion of Rome was a fully and carefully elaborated legal system. It laid down minutely the duties of man, and the fines to be paid on every transgression. It regulated the intercourse between gods and men, and showed how the good-will and co-operation of the gods could be obtained by a certain and infallible process. It was, like the civil law, full of fictions and casuistry. It imposed no obligations but those which could be accurately circumscribed by the number and quality of sacrifices and services. It suggested no such thing as love or trust or hope. The

Religion as a legal system.

notion of virtue in our sense of the word was unknown. Cicero defines piety as 'justice towards the gods,' and he adds the significant words, 'What piety is due to those from whom we have received no benefit?' It is clear that the human conscience played a very subordinate part in such a religion. Morality had nothing to do with it. Every iniquitous action was allowed by the state religion, provided a man could show that he was formally in the right. Even the gods might be cheated lawfully if a man was quick and sharp enough to avail himself of some formality in the divine law, or could interpret a doubtful injunction in his favour. An omen sent by the gods might be accepted or rejected, or interpreted in the most convenient and profitable way. A false and lying announcement by an augur had the efficacy of a true one, provided it was duly made in the prescribed form. Unlucky signs were not allowed to prevent any undertaking upon which a Roman magistrate was bent. It was only necessary to repeat the process of divination until the desired favourable signs appeared. If the entrails of the first animal were found faulty, a second was slaughtered, and a third, and so forth, until heart and liver were found to be such as foretold success. If no favourable birds would appear on the first inspection of the sky, the augur had only to continue his observations long enough, until he saw what he wished to see.

Pontiffs and other priests. The whole of this complicated system of divine law was in the keeping of the pontiffs. But neither the pontiffs nor the other priests constituted an independent power in the state. They could declare what the law was, but they could not enforce it on their own authority. They were entirely subordinate to the civil magistrates, and their principal duty was to serve the state. A conflict between the state and the priesthood was impossible. Even if the national religion had not been so intimately bound up with and dependent upon the existence of the state, the priests could not have constituted a body distinct from the rest of the community, and bound together by interests of their own. They possessed none of the conditions of such independence. They did not, like the priests of India and Egypt, form a separate caste; but they were elected for life from among the body of citizens, the high pontiff being himself generally a man of mark among the political leaders. Though not magistrates in the full sense of the word, they discharged public functions as necessary for the welfare of the state as any which were committed to the civil servants. Among these services none was more important than that of the augurs, who presided over the public auspices, the characteristic procedure by which the Roman people kept up their official intercourse with the gods. As a clear insight into the nature of the auspices is necessary for understanding the relative position of religion and the state, we must delay awhile to examine them.

Every nation of antiquity had its peculiar method for ascertaining the will of the gods. The Greeks had their oracles and dreams, the Chaldeans consulted the stars, the nations of Italy looked upon striking and unusual natural phenomena as special revelations. Thunder and lightning, earthquakes, eclipses, meteoric appearances of unexplained character or terrifying effect, abnormal or monstrous formations in men or animals, all this came under the head of 'prodigies,' awakened the 'religion,' that is the superstitious fear, of the people, and called for explanation on the part of the initiated priesthood; or, in case of necessity, for expiatory sacrifices and services. But apart from these casual manifestations of the divine will, there were methods by which men might ascertain the will of

Various forms of divination.

the gods whenever occasion required it. This was regularly done before any act or enterprise of importance, whether in private life or in the matters of state. No election, no trial, no legislative vote could take place, no war could be undertaken, no battle commenced, before the assent of the gods had been given. The gods allowed their worshippers to approach and to consult them at all times, and never refused a reply if the proper forms were employed. They sent their 'auspices' to the magistrates of the Roman people through the interposition of the augurs, who understood the nature and the meaning of the prophetic signs.

The auspices formed in some respect the very heart and centre of the practical religion of the Romans. They were the means by which every action of life was directed conformably with the divine will. Every private citizen could employ the augurs and consult the gods for his own guidance; but the magistrates alone could act on the part of the whole people and require the augurs to take public auspices. The augur on such occasions took his station in a *templum, i.e.* a consecrated plot of ground within certain defined limits; he divided the sky above him with his augural staff (the *lituus*) into four quarters, and watched for the appearance of the sacred birds sent by Jupiter. As they appeared in one or the other of the divisions he had made, so they were pronounced favourable or unfavourable. No other answer was vouchsafed by the gods, but this simple yea or nay to the question, whether the enterprise in hand was acceptable to them or not. No direction of any kind, no indication of what should be done to secure the desired end, was ever given. All this was left to the free choice of men. If they failed to adopt the right means, it was their fault; the gods did not guarantee success, but simply declared their approbation or disapprobation of the undertaking concerning which they were consulted.

This system of taking the auspices prevailed in Rome as long as the ancient religion lasted, and was only overthrown by the victory of Christianity. But it did not always continue to be animated by that spirit of faith which had given it birth. In the republican period it became gradually a mere formality. The augurs announced as the will of the gods whatever they were expected to announce; the gods were no longer allowed to put in their veto. The mode of taking the auspices was even adapted to the altered circumstances, and domestic fowls, kept in cages, were made to indicate, by their eagerness or slowness in eating, whether the gods approved or condemned an enterprise. But this indifference of later times must not mislead us with regard to the influence exercised at an early period by the auspices under the management of the priests. There can be no doubt that an unfavourable sign was in the old time a sufficient motive for abandoning any measure resolved upon by the civil power. Even the augurs themselves may be supposed to have been honest, and to have been frightened by unpropitious, or encouraged by favourable birds. They would be prevented by their own 'religion' from announcing signs which they had not really seen. Such a priesthood, firm in its own faith, exercised no doubt an influence in the state which gave to the whole scheme of government a hierarchical character. This was the character of the earliest period. Every institution of a religious nature was then in full vigour; the secular and military institutions were still in their infancy, and grew up under the shadow of the hierarchy. Law and civil policy received their impulse and first impression from religion, and only in proportion as the religious

Abuse of the auspices.

Genuine faith of the old time.

force of the national mind was spent and unable to send forth new offshoots, or even to keep life in the old roots, did the development of civil institutions take its own independent course. It is certain that after the establishment of the republic no new religious rites grew up spontaneously, whilst many of the old ones were preserved merely in outward form. We are therefore entitled to say that the **early regal period was governed chiefly by** sacerdotal **influence, and** that in it all those institutions were in full working efficiency with which we become acquainted only in the period of their decay, when they were more and more superseded by the political institutions of an age inclined to be sceptical and indifferent in religious matters.

CHAPTER VII.

CHARACTER OF THE MONARCHY.

THE chief magistrate of this age, **the king** (*rex*), **was really the high** priest **of the** nation (p. 85). He was **elected for life, not** for a term of years or an uncertain period. The man once chosen for the service of the gods was consecrated for ever, **and** this principle was applied to the priests even **after the establishment of the republic, when** the office of the civil magistrates was held for a definite period.

<small>The king was high priest.</small>

The king was, **after** his election, formally inaugurated, *i.e.* the gods were consulted by the augurs whether they approved of him as their servant. This ceremony **of** inauguration was afterwards preserved only for the pontiffs and other priests. The consuls did not require it.

<small>Inauguration of the king.</small>

But probably it was not really by popular election that the king was appointed. We know that the priests even of the republican period were not elected by the suffrages of the people, but were nominated by other priests. We may therefore infer that when the hierarchical principle was in full force, that is, in the regal period, the kings were nominated by the between-kings (*interreges*), *i.e.* by those senators who, according to a prescribed form, were selected from among the senators for the purpose of appointing a successor. *Mode of election.*

The king, we are informed, did not judge in his own person, but nominated judges (*duumviri perduellionis* and *quaestores parricidii*) to try offenders. It is quite consistent with the sacred character of a priest-king that he should not in person exercise criminal jurisdiction. *Criminal judges appointed by the king.*

It is more difficult to decide the question whether the priest-king ever took the command of the army in war. According to the traditional story Numa Pompilius, who is the type of a sacerdotal king, enjoyed perpetual peace. Perhaps the first compilers of the tales of the kings intended thereby to express the idea that it did not agree with the sacred character of the king to take the field. But if the sacerdotal king was disqualified from military command, it follows that in case of war he had to find a substitute. The question now arises whether there is any trace of magistrates who might have served as commanders of the army in the earliest period of Roman history. *Military commanders.*

In historical times we often hear of the appointment of Dictators in times of extraordinary dangers. We are told that they were anciently called Masters of the people (*Magistri populi*), and we also hear of the office of Chief Praetor (*praetor maximus*), which appears to have been identical with that of master of the people. The custom of appointing masters of the people or chief praetors certainly preceded the establishment of the republic. It is not unlikely therefore that they were the officers who in the time of the sacerdotal kings took the command of the army. The dictators were not elected by popular suffrage, like the other republican magistrates. They were nominated by one of the consuls, and after nomination they had to assemble the people and to obtain their promise of obedience. This process of appointment appears to date from pre-republican times, and we may perhaps venture to say that a similar process was adopted on the appointment of the ancient masters of the people, that the sacerdotal king nominated them when occasion required, and that they obtained the formal sanction of the people by a resolution which pledged the people to acknowledge their authority.

If this was the constitutional process in the regal period, we can easily imagine how it came to pass that the old sacerdotal king was superseded by a military monarch (p. 85). We need only suppose that a *magister populi*, favoured by circumstances, refused to lay down the power lodged in his hands. The temporary chief of the army would thus become a ruler for life, and the constitution of the state would be changed. But in all probability the revolution resulted not in a violent abolition of all existing institutions. It was in some respects a development and consolidation of certain pre-existing elements, and it was a decided progress. It strengthened the internal unity of the state, abolished the remnants of the old federal system, toned down the undue prominence of the religious element and the predominance of the priests, and brought out the national strength by organising a new

Sacerdotal kings superseded by military chiefs.

popular assembly and a new army. It destroyed the exclusive privilege of a ruling class of noble houses, and thus laid the foundations upon which, with very few changes, the republic could be established.

By the side of the old sacerdotal king there was evidently no room for another chief of the national religion. There could have been no high pontiff at the time when a priest-king like Numa presided over the religious institutions of the people. This inference is borne out by the legendary account. Numa is related to have appointed a pontifex of the name of Numa Marcius. This Numa Marcius is evidently no other person than Numa Pompilius himself, for the addition of the second name is in this case, as in many others, nothing but a feeble attempt of the annalists to make two persons out of one. Moreover the identity of pontifex and king in the old time is sufficiently proved by the fact that the ancient palace of the king, the *regia*, was at the same time the official dwelling of the pontifex maximus.

<small>Pontiffs appointed after the abolition of the sacerdotal royalty.</small>

This identity of king and pontiff could only last as long as the king was essentially a priest and the head of the national religion. When a military chief usurped the supreme power the old sacerdotal king must have been stripped of his political authority. It was most probably by this revolution that the pontifical duties were separated from the political and transferred to a purely sacerdotal officer, the pontifex. The military king could no more take upon himself the exercise of all the purely sacerdotal functions than in an earlier period the priest-king could have commanded the army. A new arrangement was made. The priests were made dependent on the magistrates, and religion became the handmaid of politics.

Thus it was that the primeval policy of Rome, which was essentially religious or sacerdotal, passed over into a military monarchy. When at a later stage the monarchy was overthrown, the old institutions were not re-established, but the republican magistrates stepped into the place of the military kings, and religion lost more and more the influence which it had once possessed. The title and office of priest-king *(rex sacrorum)* was indeed preserved, for religious scruples forbade their formal abolition, but this 'king of the sacrifices' was debarred from all political influence. He was not allowed to hold any civil office, and even in his own peculiar department he was made subordinate to the chief pontiff.

CHAPTER VIII.

THE SENATE OF THE REGAL PERIOD.

IF in the earliest constitution of Rome the king was rather the head of the national religion than a chief executive officer, it follows that the community required some other central authority invested with political power, able to bind together the federative elements of which the state consisted, and to direct the government. This authority was lodged in the senate, a body of men consisting of all or the most influential heads of families, and therefore appropriately called 'fathers' *(patres)*. They must have formed a kind of representative assembly, although the idea of representation in the modern sense was foreign to the whole ancient world. If it is reported that Romulus chose at first one hundred men to be senators, that this number was doubled on the union with the

The fathers de facto representatives of the great houses.

Sabines, and that under Tarquin one hundred more were added, we understand that the earliest annalists considered three hundred to have been the normal number of senators, and that this number was reached gradually. Now this number agreed with the division of the people in the prehistoric time, viz., the three tribes (Ramnes, Tities, and Luceres), divided into thirty curies, and (probably) three hundred gentes or houses. It would appear, therefore, that the ancient senate was intended to contain a member of each of the houses, and in so far these houses were in fact all 'represented' in the senate.

If that was so, it seems that the individual members could hardly have been freely chosen by the king, as in republican times they were by the consuls, and afterwards by the censors. It would seem more natural that each house had a right to be represented in the senate by its head (*pater*), though probably the formal nomination may have been the king's privilege or duty.

As a consequence of this inherent right of the heads of houses to form the senate, it would naturally follow that the senate was not merely, as it was in republican times, a consultative body, but that it would share to a certain extent the executive government of the state. This we may moreover infer from certain formal rights which the republican senate retained, and which were probably only the remnants of rights more real and extensive of older date. We know that the consent called 'authority of the fathers' (*patrum auctoritas*) was required for all elections and all legislative acts of the people. This right may be presumed to have been of much more importance in the earlier period.

<small>The authority of the fathers.</small>

A second privilege of the senate in republican times was the right of deciding when a dictator should be named.

It seems a safe conclusion that, in the time of the sacerdotal kings, it was in like manner the senate which determined when a *magister populi* should be elected to take the military command.

But the most significant remnant of ancient prerogative possessed by the senators even in historical times was the right of acting as *interreges* (between-kings) *i.e.* of taking upon themselves the executive power in the *interregnum*, the interval between the death of duly elected magistrates and the installation of their successors. Such an event would more rarely happen in the time of the republic, when two chief magistrates were annually appointed; but it regularly occurred in the regal period on the death of a king. Then it was that the senate as a body stepped into the king's place, one senator after another acting as 'interrex' for five days, until a new king was appointed. At such times the right to take the auspices which had been possessed by the deceased king passed over to the body of the senators. These men stood forward now as the mediators between the Roman gods and the Roman people; they took care that the link was not broken between the two, that the auspices could be duly taken, and that, with the consent of the gods, a new king should be appointed.

The interregnum.

The senate, therefore, occupied a most influential position under the sacerdotal kings. When the revolution took place, which placed military kings at the head of the state, we hear of conflicts between them and the senate. The younger Tarquin is said to have expelled and even murdered many senators, and to have in fact superseded the senate altogether. He was not nominated in due form by an interrex, and was therefore, according to the spirit of the ancient public law, a usurper not entitled to take the public auspices of the Roman people. When he was ex-

Conflict between the senate and the later kings.

pelled, the power of the senate revived, and new senators were appointed in place of those whom Tarquin had killed. In fact, a regular aristocratic restoration took place. The liberty gained by the downfall of the tyrant was not a liberty for the lower classes of citizens, but a liberty for the nobility, who exercised their power in a spirit so hostile to the people that the Tarquins were looked upon with tender regret. The people were soon driven to rise against their oppressors, and to force them to concessions by seceding in a body to the Sacred Hill, and threatening to separate themselves from Rome.

The secession to the Sacred Hill was the commencement of the growth of popular liberties. To understand it we must examine the condition of the people in the preceding period.

CHAPTER IX.

THE PEOPLE IN THE REGAL PERIOD.

THE Roman people were not a homogeneous mass. Apart from actual slaves, who were never classed with the people in any ancient community, we observe two distinct classes of citizens, the patricians and the plebeians, *i.e.* the ruling class of citizens in the possession of the full franchise, and an inferior dependent class. A similar distinction between two classes of citizens we find in every state of antiquity. It owes its origin to conquest and to the necessity under which the conquerors found themselves of admitting the conquered races to some sort of civil fellowship. The rule was, that the inferior class were allowed to enjoy certain private rights of property and personal security. They were not slaves in the full sense of the word; for slaves

The people. Patricians & plebeians.

never enjoyed the **protection of** the law for either **property** or life. But the conquered race was not admitted to civil equality with the conquerors. They had to bear the civil burdens in return for the protection they enjoyed; they **had especially to** join their rulers **in the** defence of the common country; but they were **excluded** from the **political** rights of the sovereign people, *i.e.* from a voice in **the national assemblies,** whether for the election of magistrates, **or for** resolutions **affecting the** national policy, or for legislation, or finally, for the trial of offenders.

All **these functions** accordingly devolved in **Rome** exclusively on the patricians, *i.e.* the members of those families who had founded the state by conquest. They alone formed what was anciently called the 'populus Romanus' in opposition to the plebs. This patrician populus was divided into tribes, curiae, and gentes. The assembly of curies (*comitia curiata*) was consequently an assembly of patricians only; at least, it seems clear that plebeians, if admitted to listen or to be present when the curies met, took no active part in their decisions.

<small>Patrician assembly of curiae.</small>

The comitia curiata were the only popular assemblies **known** in the earliest period, when the national institutions bore a pre-eminently religious character, and the original confederacy had not yet been fully developed into **a real** state with a centralized, secular government. The assembly **voted by curies,** that is, there were thirty votes, all the members of one **curia uniting to form one vote.** The king presided, **and all** questions of national importance were here decided, viz., the election (or perhaps only the inauguration) of kings, **the** investment of a commander with military power (*the lex curiata de imperio*), declarations of war, the trial of offenders, and finally the adoption of laws, if formal legislation can be supposed to have taken place at that time.

The constitution of Rome exhibits with regard to popular assemblies a feature not found anywhere else. It is this, that not less than three different forms of such assemblies existed side by side differently organized and having each its own peculiar functions. The assembly of curies, of which we have just spoken, was the oldest and for a time the only assembly. In the second period of the kings was organized the military assembly of centuries, which was destined chiefly for the election of military commanders for decisions about peace and war and for the trial of those citizens who had broken the peace and were therefore looked upon as public enemies. The third form of assemblies, the *comitia tributa*, was introduced in consequence of the rising of the plebs. They included only plebeians, and were at first confined to the election of plebeian magistrates (the tribunes of the people and the plebeian aediles) and to questions concerning the plebs alone. But in course of time this last assembly acquired more and more importance, and was invested with the character of a national assembly. The peculiar organization of these three assemblies constitutes the distinguishing feature of the three successive periods of the Roman constitution. We shall become acquainted with the centuriate assembly when we come to review the republican government in its oldest form, and with the assemblies of tribes when we examine the rise and progress of the tribunician power. Of the curiatic assembly we need say no more than that as far as real life and influence are concerned it was a thing of the past when Rome emerged from the prehistoric period. It was then one of those unmeaning forms which the Romans preserved from their national veneration for old institutions, and which enable the historian to form an opinion of times otherwise buried in utter oblivion.

The three different popular assemblies.

The patricians, as we have seen, formed the ruling body. By the side of them there existed from the earliest times a subordinate class called plebeians, enjoying indeed the name of Roman citizens and entitled to the protec-

<small>Rights of the plebeians.</small> tion of life and property, differing therefore widely from slaves, but still excluded from a share in the government, from the senate, the assembly of curies, the auspices of the state, and from intermarriage with the patricians. They thus formed a distinct body, a subject population bound to bear the burdens of the state without sharing in its government. They had no doubt a separate organization to manage their own affairs, their peculiar sanctuaries, their assemblies, religious and social, their own officers for administrative and judicial purposes. But of these things we can only form conjectures, based upon the institutions of a later period, as no satisfactory evidence can be traced back to the period of the kings.

Nor are we better informed of the origin of the plebeians. According to the traditional story, it was <small>Origin of the plebs.</small> Romulus who by his own will and pleasure divided the whole mass of citizens into patricians and plebeians. This account is no more to be trusted than the stories of the legislation of Romulus and Numa. Dependent classes are not made by legislators; they are the result of political revolutions. The Roman plebeians must have been the descendants of a population reduced to subjection by conquest. But when and how this was done is beyond the reach of our knowledge. It is possible that the original population of the country was at one time conquered by an invading host of new settlers and then reduced to the condition of plebeians; it is possible also that the invaders brought with them a class of dependents, the result of a previous conquest. We cannot speculate on these possibilities with any prospect of profit, and must rest satisfied with a general impression rendered plausible by analogy.

A certain number of plebeians were distinguished from the rest by the name of clients. These clients appear to have been attached as hereditary dependents to certain patrician families. Each patrician had a number, of whom he was called the 'patron.' He was bound specially to watch over their interests, and to act as their legal protector, whilst in return they paid him fixed dues and services. *The clients.*

The clients seem to have played an important part in the early period. They are often mentioned as the special partisans of the patricians in their disputes with the plebs. They would appear therefore to have been practically a distinct class of citizens, although the law knew only patricians and plebeians, and classed the clients among the latter. In course of time the difference between clients and other plebeians disappeared. The old clientship became a thing of the past, and was replaced by a new clientship of a somewhat different order, with which the early history of Rome has no concern.

It is not at all unlikely that the condition of the plebeians was improved by the military kings, who limited the power of the more aristocratic form of government in which the heads of patrician houses, assembled in the senate, ruled the state under the nominal control of a sacerdotal king. The establishment of the comitia centuriata, which first gave political rights to the plebeians, is ascribed to Servius Tullius. The Tarquins, who are represented as hostile to the nobility, must have relied upon the support of the plebeians, and we are told that upon the expulsion of the kings the patricians were compelled to make concessions to the plebeians, in order to *The military kings the patrons of the plebs.*

reconcile them to the republican government. We are told, moreover, that as soon as all danger of a restoration of the kings was past, the patricians showed themselves less conciliatory to the plebeians, and that the latter were thus forced into an open rebellion, which threatened the state with dissolution and was only brought to an end by fresh concessions on the part of the patricians. This rebellion is the famous secession to the Sacred Hill, the starting-point of plebeian liberties, to which we shall soon have to turn our attention.

CHAPTER X.

THE MAGISTRATES OF THE REPUBLIC.

IT would be a great mistake to look upon the republican institutions, established after the fall of the Tarquin monarchy, as an entirely new creation. We have already had occasion to observe that such new creations are unknown in the history of the human race, and that all that appears to be new in constitutional reforms is in fact only a development of existing germs. This can be satisfactorily shown to have been the case at Rome, in this early period of its career, as it was at every subsequent stage.

The division of the people into patricians and plebeians remained what it had been. The patrician assembly of curies retained its religious character; the military and political assembly of centuries came into regular working order; the Senate continued to be the great council of the nation, but a change was made in the executive. In the place of a king for life two annual chief magistrates

Change in the executive.

were appointed under the name of 'praetors,' which name was afterwards changed into that of 'consuls.' To these annual magistrates the power of the kingly office was transferred undiminished, as were also the insignia of the kings. The change seemed slight; yet it was most important. For by the limitation of the office to a short period of time, the Romans secured the personal responsibility of their chief magistrates, which is the most essential part of republican government. During his term of office a magistrate could not have been subject to a criminal prosecution and punishment without derogating from the majesty of the state, as represented by him, and without danger to the safety of the republic itself. But his term of office being over, the consul became a private citizen, and was amenable to the laws. This prospect of an impending settlement of accounts was calculated to keep an annual magistrate in the path of duty, whilst a king who retained power as long as he lived was free from such salutary considerations. *The consular office. Limited in time.*

The second modification in the office of chief magistrate was its partition among two colleagues, equal in every respect in rank and power. This measure, which necessarily impaired to some extent the unity and vigour of the executive, was adopted as a precaution against the abuse of authority. Not satisfied with the limitation of the office to a short annual period, the Romans desired a guarantee for their liberty even during that period, and they expected to find it in the control which one consul might exercise over the other. Each of them was entrusted consequently with the right of 'intercession,' *i.e.* he could place his veto on any official act of his colleague. Such a right might of course be abused to the great detriment of the public interest; but coupled with *Its partition among two colleagues. Right of intercession.*

the responsibility which awaited every consul after the expiration of his term of office, it proved on the whole so successful that the Romans adhered to it cheerfully through all the vicissitudes of their history, until the republican government passed into a monarchy.

However, they were not blind to the weakness of the arrangement, which they had adopted out of jealousy for their liberties. Whenever it was found that the division of authority endangered the national independence, in great emergencies of foreign or domestic conflicts, they had recourse to a temporary restoration of undivided authority, by appointing a single chief officer, called Dictator, to supersede the two consuls, and to unite in his own hands the whole executive power as it had been possessed by the kings.

The dictatorship.

A dictator was appointed after a decree of the senate, not by popular suffrage, but by one of the consuls, who, although nominally free in his choice, would naturally name the man pointed out by the general confidence as equal to the occasion. The consent of the people to his nomination was expressed by a solemn act of the assembly of curies (not the centuries), which being summoned by the dictator himself, conferred upon him (by the so-called *lex curiata*) the 'Imperium,' *i.e.* the chief and unlimited military command. The dictator then appointed an officer second in command, called 'Master of the Horse' (*magister equitum*), to act under his orders. The consuls and all other magistrates were suspended during the time the dictator carried on the government, and they re-entered on their offices the moment he abdicated. This he did as soon as the emergency which had called for his nomination was over, the maximum term of his office being six months.

Our authorities are not agreed as to the time when the dictatorship was first established, nor as to the name of the first man who filled the office. They agree in so far that it belongs to the first period of the republic. It is, in all likelihood, of still higher antiquity; in fact, those officers who led the legions of Rome in the earliest times, in the age of the sacerdotal kings, were probably dictators or the prototypes of dictators. We have already (p. 102) pointed out the probability that the official names 'master of the people' (*magister populi*) and 'first praetor' (*praetor maximus*), which are reported to have been synonymous with the title of dictator, were used to designate these chief officers in the pre-republican age. They were certainly not used afterwards, and as they were titles of high antiquity, we are led to assume that they were applied to a constitutional office in the oldest period of Rome.

<small>Origin of the dictatorship.</small>

If this conjecture prove correct, we see that the republican practice was also in this respect far from being an entire novelty, and that the forms of the republican institutions were partly a revival, partly a development of a former state of things. We may go further and say, that in all probability the duality of the chief office, *i.e.* the consular form of government, was probably not introduced immediately upon the expulsion of the kings, but that that event was followed in the first instance by the restoration of the dictatorship, which in its turn was modified to give place to the consular government.

Such a course of events is made highly probable by the traditions which clung to the name of Valerius Poplicola. It is related that after the death of Brutus, his colleague, in the first year of the republic (p. 60), he remained alone in office as sole consul, and omitted to call an assembly of the people for the election of a second consul. This proceeding, it

<small>Valerius Poplicola.</small>

is said, gave umbrage to the people, especially as Valerius began to build himself a house on the Velia, the very spot where the kings had resided. It was feared that he was about to imitate the example of Tarquin, and aspire to make himself sole and perpetual master. But Valerius put to shame all fear and all suspicion. He proposed and passed a law in the centuriate assembly, by which it was declared high treason in a citizen to assume public authority which was not legally and freely conferred upon him by the people; in other words, a law punishing by outlawry and confiscation any attempt to restore the monarchy. A second law of Valerius granted to every citizen the right of appeal from a penal sentence of the magistrates to the popular assembly. These two laws contained the formal abolition of the monarchy, and secured the acknowledgment of the sovereignty of the people. To mark this by an outward sign, Valerius ordered the axes to be removed from the fasces of his lictors, and thus appeared before the people without the dreaded instruments of death, which had been a significant part of the royal and dictatorial insignia. From this time forward the consuls did not show the axes within the precincts of the city. This symbol of power over life and death was reserved to the dictators, and in case of war to the consuls in the field.

The Valerian laws.

The tradition of the policy of Valerius deserves credit inasmuch as it was necessarily kept alive by the continued enforcement of the Valerian laws, the charter of the republic. It points unmistakeably to the fact that the annual election of two magistrates, which is the characteristic mark of the republic, was preceded by a period in which not two, but one man was at the head of the state, and that the time of office was not then strictly limited to one year. This dictatorship, again, was not a new invention, but the revival of the old, or perhaps, primeval office of an occasional 'master of the people,' which had degenerated in the time of the Tarquins into government for life.

The duties of government in the states of antiquity were very simple, especially in states so small and so little advanced in civilisation as Rome was in the earlier stages of her career. The principal duty devolving upon the consuls was the command of the army in those everlasting petty wars in which Rome, like every small and rude community, was involved. To maintain the independence of the state is the primary object of all national institutions, and the military organisation was therefore the foundation for all civil order; the army, as we shall see, was the model for the popular assembly. *Duties of the consular office.*

Internal peace, not less important than protection from abroad, was secured by the laws, and here again the duties of the Roman magistrates were very simple. For the settlement of private disputes and claims, private arbitrators agreed upon by the parties acted under the authority and sanction of the magistrates. Criminal jurisdiction alone was in the hands of the magistrates; but the consuls could (like the kings) appoint judges (quaestors) for the trial of offenders. An appeal lay from the decision of the magistrate to the popular assembly, which was thus constituted the highest court of law in criminal jurisdiction. *Administration of justice.*

The public jurisdiction was to a considerable extent limited by the private jurisdiction exercised by every paterfamilias over the members of his family and his slaves. As he had power of life and death, it may easily be imagined how important this family jurisdiction must have been. *Private jurisdiction.*

Religion being in Rome, as everywhere in antiquity,

a political and national institution, and therefore necessarily under the control of the state, the priests and other ministers of religion were to a certain extent public servants; though they differed from the secular magistrates in being appointed not by the people but by other priests, and not for a limited term, but for life. They were not confined to their priestly functions. They might hold civil offices, and it could and did happen that even the chief pontiff, the head of the national worship, was praetor or consul. The king of sacrifices (*rex sacrorum*) was the solitary exception. He was not only lowered in authority, being placed under the chief pontiff, though nominally first in rank, but he was specially debarred from all public functions, civil or military. His office was preserved only as a relic of past times, and this is among the most noteworthy examples of that superstitious conservatism which made the Romans scruple formally to abolish old institutions, even when they were superseded in reality. This tendency is especially perceptible when the old institutions were sanctioned by religion, introduced by auspices with the special approbation of the gods, and connected with solemn periodical rites, as was the case with the office of the king of sacrifices.

<small>The priests public servants.</small>

The office of pontiff was by far the most important of all those connected with religion. The pontiffs, three in number (afterwards seven), with a high pontiff (*pontifex maximus*) at their head, were not priests in the strict sense of the word, not being specially attached to the service of any particular god. They were rather a body of superintendents, guardians of the purity of the national religion and worship, interpreters of the divine law; and as the divine law (*fas*) was the foundation of civil law, they were in

<small>The pontiffs the interpreters of divine and human law;</small>

possession of all those forms and technicalities which constituted a most essential feature in Roman jurisprudence, and the exclusive knowledge of which was doubly valuable at a time when the laws were not committed to writing but jealously watched as a sacred and secret treasure. In the maze of numberless and subtle intricacies which the complicated system of religious observances could not fail to present, the people, whether in their private capacity or as public servants, were obliged constantly to have recourse to the pontiffs, who would advise them what solemn words had to be spoken, what times and seasons to be observed, what gestures and dress, what purifications and sacrifices were necessary to avert the anger of a deity ever ready to avenge the least, even involuntary, deviation from the prescribed rule. When a word wrongfully omitted or added, or an omen misinterpreted or neglected, might possibly bring irretrievable ruin on a worshipper, and could at any rate be expiated only by a certain definite rite or sacrifice, the advice of the pontiffs must have been in constant request, and their influence must have been unbounded.

Besides the strictly religious duties which they had to discharge, the pontiffs represented in some sense the science and literature of the nation, like the Christian clergy amid the universal ignorance of the middle ages. They were the public astronomers, having to fix the solemn days for worship and political transactions, to divide the year into months and weeks, to keep it in accordance with the course of the sun, a duty which they discharged with reckless irregularity, partly from ignorance, partly to serve political and party purposes. They were also, as we have seen (page 21), the national chroniclers, and as such were bound to cultivate what might be called a literature.

and the guardians of science and learning.

But their annals were no great literary performance, and the literature of Rome remained in a rudimentary condition, until Greek influence made itself felt.

The public auspices were in the keeping of another body of religious functionaries, the Augurs, who like the pontiffs were not really priests in the strict sense of the word, as they had not to conduct any public worship. Their only duty was to assist the magistrates in taking the auspices, *i.e.* to act as their servants, when they wished to consult the will of the gods. They could not act of their own accord, but had to wait till they were bidden. They were therefore far from being able to exercise an independent authority or to counteract and thwart the public will. The signs sent by the gods were sent not to them, but to the magistrates. All that the augurs had to do was to watch for them in the form prescribed by the sacred law, to interpret and to announce them to the magistrates; and the spirit of formalism pervading the religion of Rome was such, that if an augur by mistake or purposely announced signs which he had not seen, the magistrate was justified in acting upon the announcement as if it had been correct, and the gods were supposed to be bound by the false announcement, though they might punish the augur for making it.

The system of public auspices sprung up, like every religious custom, in a period of unbounded faith, at a time when no man would have ventured upon any enterprise, unless he had honestly ascertained by undoubted signs the will of the approving deity. But this faith did not survive long the primeval period of sacerdotal kings. After the establishment of the republic the auspices began to be used as a political instrument to serve purely political ends. The science of the augurs was pressed into the service of the state, and they were made to announce favourable or unfavourable auspices as the public interest or even the interest of a party might require. The election of political adversaries might thus be frustrated on the pretext that the auspices were against it; a law might be rejected on the same plea, an expedition postponed or given up, a consul called back from a campaign, in short any measure annulled or thwarted by this means without making it appear that political considerations dictated the opposition. Of course such procedures would in the end dull the edge of the weapon employed. People will not submit to be influenced by religious scruples when they discover that their scruples are not shared by priests or rulers, who make good use of them for worldly purposes. This was shown at Rome in the contest between the patricians and the plebeians. The clenching argument of the former was always this, that the plebeians could not take the auspices and therefore could not hold the high offices of state. When the plebeians had gradually acquired power and influence enough to extort equal political rights from their opponents, this argument was found to be based on false assumptions, for no difficulty was experienced by plebeian consuls, when they had to approach the gods through the old patrician auspices.

CHAPTER XI.

THE SENATE OF THE REPUBLIC.

'THE Senate and the people of Rome' (*S.P.Q.R.*, i.e. *senatus populusque Romanus*) was the official designation of the Roman commonwealth. The precedence occupied in this title by the senate is indicative of the prominence of that assembly in the public life of Rome. The senate was indeed the soul of that mighty body. The greatness of Rome is to be ascribed not so much to the eminent genius of a few men, nor to the civic virtues and martial spirit of the people, as to the ability displayed at all times by this assembly, which united within itself whatever of worth or talent, of experience and political wisdom the whole nation possessed.

The senate had neither executive, nor legislative, nor judicial power. It was merely a consultative body free to give advice to the magistrates, when asked for it, but unable either to give advice unasked or to enforce its acceptance. Its influence consisted in this, that it really represented the intelligence of the people, and generally gave a correct expression of the national will.

<small>The senate a consultative body.</small>

The normal number of senators is supposed to have been three hundred in the kingly period (see p. 105). They were of course all patricians. The last king is said to have reduced the senate in numbers and to have disregarded its advice. On the establishment of the republic the senate regained its old position. Brutus, or, according to other statements, Valerius added many new senators, and thus restored the former standard. Our informants are of opinion that these new senators were taken from among the plebeians; and whilst some think that they were by their nomination raised to the rank of patricians, others fancy that they remained plebeians— that the senate, therefore, from the commencement of the republic contained a considerable number of plebeian members. This is, however, a notion which cannot be entertained. It is refuted by all that we know of the early constitutional struggles between patricians and plebeians. The plebeians were for a long time after in a depressed condition, excluded from all participation in the government of the republic. It took them a cen-

<small>Number of senators.</small>

<small>New senators added after the expulsion of Tarquin were not plebeians.</small>

tury and a half before they were admitted to the consulship, and two hundred years elapsed before they were declared eligible for any priestly offices. Up to 445 B.C. they were excluded from intermarriage with the **patricians**. When after a severe struggle and an armed insurrection tribunes of the plebs were created, to act as patrons of the plebeians and to ward off the worst **form of** oppression, these tribunes were not allowed access to the senate, but had for a long time to take **their** seats outside the sacred precincts **and to shout their interceding ' veto '** through the open door. How is it credible that **such an** assembly should **have** received a number **of plebeian** members in the **very first year of the republic**? To believe such an extraordinary statement, we should require better evidence than we have.

But even supposing that **Brutus or Valerius** completed the number of senators **from** the plebs, these **new** plebeian members must have died in course of time, and therefore, **if no law was enacted to** provide for plebeian successors, **the senate would in a short** time have become **purely** patrician again. Of such a **law we** have no trace, nor is it reported that the alleged act of Brutus or Valerius was ever repeated. We hear of no election of plebeian senators, nor of the presence of plebeians in the senate during the early period of the republic. **The** senate is constantly **represented** as the champion of the patrician order, without a dissentient voice. **It is there**fore an absolute impossibility that **plebeians should have** been received into it at the time in **question**.

The arguments adduced against the possible reception of plebeians into the senate by Brutus or Valerius do not tell with equal force against the assumption that plebeians were indeed received, but **were** at the same time raised to patrician rank. **Yet even** this seems improbable, for such a **precedent** as the wholesale creation of a number of new patrician families from the body of plebeians could not have failed to be followed in after times, and would have led to drafting off the foremost leaders of the plebeians into the patrician ranks. It would have been such a weakening of the plebeian opposition that the struggle would have lost its asperity and tradition would not have failed to commemorate some instances of transition from the lower to the higher order of citizens. But not a single instance is alleged. Nay, it appears to have been impossible in law. We are therefore compelled to assume that the new senators created by Brutus or Valerius were members of patrician houses.

<small>Nor were the new members plebeians raised to the rank of patricians.</small>

This assumption agrees with all that we know of the subsequent history. It is certain that the revolution which overthrew the kings led to a restoration of aristocratic, *i.e.* patrician government. It was a revolution not in favour of the people, *i.e.* the mass of the lower ranks, but, as we have already remarked, it was rather directed against their interests. The plebeians were so far from being benefited by it, that they had to rise in open rebellion, to obtain, not equality with the patricians, not a share in the government, but simple protection from arbitrary and illegal treatment. The senate during this time and for a long time after was most assuredly patrician throughout, and had never been tainted by the presence even of ennobled plebeians.

<small>The senate purely patrician and champion of patrician interests.</small>

The new senators added by Brutus or Valerius are said to have been called *conscripti*, in distinction from the older members, who were simply called *patres*. Thus, it is said, arose the title *patres conscripti*, conscript fathers, which was the official designation of the Roman senators, for *patres*

<small>The title *patres conscripti*.</small>

conscripti, we are told, is contracted from *patres et conscripti*. This explanation of the name falls to the ground with the assumption that the new members differed in rank from the older. It is an attempt of some antiquarian to account for the peculiar title of the senate, and cannot be based upon a genuine tradition. We must explain the title differently. We know (what not all the annalists knew) that the word *patres* meant originally not senators, but members of the patrician community as distinct from the plebeians. Hence not all the *patres*, in strictness of speech the *lords* or masters of families, were senators, and to distinguish the latter from the body of *patres*, they were called *patres conscripti*, *i.e.* fathers whose names were 'entered' (*conscripta*) on the lists of the senators.

The Roman senate was a consultative body of men picked from the mass of the community and accustomed to meet periodically for the discussion of public affairs. It resembled therefore in many respects the representative assemblies of modern times, and upon the whole exercised a similar influence upon the direction of affairs. But in detail the difference is perhaps more striking than the resemblance; and as we are too apt to form our ideas of the past from the analogies of the present, it is worth while to notice some of the most striking features in which the Roman senate differed from modern parliaments.

<small>Difference of the senate from modern parliaments.</small>

The senate was not a representative assembly in the strict sense of the word. The members were not elected by the suffrage of the people; nor did they sit and vote for particular divisions of the nation or territory. They were nominated by the executive government, *i.e.* by the consuls, and after the establishment of the censorship (in 443 B.C.)

<small>The senate not a representative assembly.</small>

by the censors. Only in a limited degree and in an indirect way had the people any influence in the nomination of senators, inasmuch as they elected the electors, and as the latter were bound to call into the senate men who enjoyed the confidence of the people, in the first instance, therefore, men who had discharged public offices. In the earlier period of the republic, when the two consuls were the only annual magistrates, the vacancies in the senate caused by death could not all be filled up by ex-magistrates; and even when the number of annual magistrates was considerably increased, the senate could only be kept at its normal standard by the nomination of men who had not previously discharged a public office. Yet those senators who had passed the official chairs were always the leaders in the senate, and it appears that the other senators had only the right to vote and not that of justifying their vote by set speeches.

<small>Mode of electing senators.</small>

As the senators held their seats for life, or at least during good behaviour, and as the senate accordingly was never renewed *in toto* by a dissolution, it constituted a permanent, undying body, only receiving fresh blood from time to time, as old men dropped off and others were substituted in their place. They may, in short, be said to have held life peerages. This circumstance naturally gave to the senate the character of great stability and decided conservatism. New ideas could make their way but slowly in such an assembly, and the people had no means of pushing measures of reform through a body which could not, like a modern parliament, be reconstructed on new principles at a general election.

<small>Character of stability of the senate.</small>

At the same time, the traditions of bygone times, the constitutional precedents, which in the absence of a written constitution contained the public law of the republic, could not be better preserved in their purity than by such an assembly. If we take into consideration that not only the consuls after their year of office, but also pontiffs and other priests were life members of the senate, we can understand how the knowledge of many old institutions, and even a dim recollection of the events that led to their establishment, might be recorded and handed down for generations before it was consigned to writing.

CHAPTER XII.

THE POPULAR ASSEMBLIES OF THE REPUBLIC.

THE senate, as we have seen, had no direct influence on the election of magistrates or on legislative enactments. These powers were lodged in the assembly of the people, and constituted the attributes of sovereignty, which in the ancient republics the people never delegated to any person or select body, but invariably reserved to themselves as an inalienable right. *The proper functions of the popular assemblies.*

The oldest form of a popular assembly in Rome was, as we have seen (pp. 35, 108), that of the curies (*comitia curiata*). It consisted of patricians alone, to the exclusion of plebeians. This assembly was never formally abolished, but in republican times it had lost all real political power, and was retained only for the sake of a few formalities more of a religious than a political character, of which the most remarkable was the annual passing of the law *de imperio*, which conferred the military command on every newly elected consul, and thus resembled in some way the annual enactment of the mutiny bill in England. *The comitia curiata superseded.*

When Roman history emerges from the legendary

period we find another form of popular assembly in operation, the 'assembly of centuries' (*comitia centuriata*), organised on an entirely different plan. The plebeians were no longer excluded, nor was family relationship and descent the principle of classification. The whole people, patricians and plebeians, were divided into five classes according to a property qualification, and each of these five classes was subdivided into a certain number of voting units, called centuries the first class having eighty, each of the three succeeding classes twenty centuries, and the last class thirty, thus making up a total of 170 centuries or votes. In addition to these there were eighteen centuries of knights and four centuries of musicians, smiths, and carpenters, which were formed without regard to the amount of their property. The qualification of the members of the first class was, according to the statement of Livy, the possession of property valued above 100,000 *asses*, or pounds of copper. In each successive class this figure was less by 25,000 *asses*, so that the fifth class embraced the citizens owning less than 25,000 *asses* (page 50). There are, indeed, many controverted points of detail, arising from the fact that our informants differ from one another; but as they agree in the general character of the arrangement, we need not here be detained by these variations.

The comitia centuriata.

It must strike everyone at first sight that this is a division of the people on military principles. The people, in fact, was here looked upon as an army and divided into fighting bodies. The 170 centuries of the five classes were all infantry; the cavalry was formed by the eighteen centuries of knights; the musicians and engineers were equally essential branches of the service. Then each class consisted of an equal number of young fighting men, and of veterans, the

Military character of the comitia centuriata.

former destined to take the field, the latter reserved for the defence of the city. The men of the higher classes were bound to provide themselves with more or less complete armour; the lower classes were light-armed; and the horses for the cavalry were furnished by the state. Lastly, the place of meeting for this assembly was the field of Mars, and the signal for calling it together was not the voice of the public crier but the military trumpet.

From all this it is evident that the original purpose of the centuriate assembly was to provide protection for the state by organizing the whole body of citizens as an army. It followed as a natural consequence that this body was entrusted with the decisions of peace and war and with the election of commanders, the two most important matters for every state and almost the only questions which would be of frequent occurrence in a rude community situated like that of Rome. Criminal offenders were looked upon as enemies of the country and were, very properly, tried by the same body which fought against foreign enemies. The final decision in legislative questions thus fell within the competency of the same military assembly of centuries, which thus became the sovereign assembly of the Roman people. *Functions of the comitia.*

But how did it first arise? Our informants are ready with a very simple answer. They affirm that one of the kings, called Servius Tullius, worked out the plan in his own brain, finished it in all its detail, and was about to introduce it when he was murdered by Tarquin, the tyrant; that during the reign of Tarquin the scheme of Servius remained unexecuted, and that on his expulsion the Romans drew it forth from the public archives and made it the foundation of their new republican form of government. *Alleged origin of the comitia curiata.*

We need hardly say that this cannot have been the

A. H.   K

way in which the centuriate comitia came into being, and supplanted the curies. This change can have come to pass only in consequence of a revolution which changed the old sacerdotal kingdom into a military monarchy, breaking up the primeval federal constitution with its three tribes of Ramnes, Tities, and Luceres, its thirty curies, its patrician houses and their clients, and raising the plebeians from their degraded position to the rank of Roman citizens. By this revolution Rome became a military power, and even when the kings were expelled, the military organization of the people created by them was retained and no doubt contributed to give Rome a superiority over her neighbours. The memory of the process which led to this great advance has been lost. Whether it was entirely worked out by an internal organic reform, or whether Etruscan rulers introduced it, cannot now be proved by any external evidence. Some few traces in the traditions point to the latter alternative; for instance, the account of the opposition which the elder Tarquin met when he wished to reform the old centuries of knights (page 46). The native Sabine augur Attus Navius, we are told, resisted the foreign king, but was obliged to yield when Tarquin, though reforming the old institutions, left the old names unaltered. Servius Tullius, the traditional author of the centuriate comitia, is represented in some annals as an Etruscan warrior named Mastarna, coming to Rome and settling there with his followers. These are indications of a reform caused by foreign influence. Yet there are not wanting traces which seem to show that the centuriate organization was an organic development of that of the curies— a theory which, however, does not exclude the possibility of foreign influence to facilitate and direct the process.

The popular assembly could only meet when duly convoked by a consul on a day set apart by the pontifical calendar for such meetings. Under the presidency of a consul the people were called upon to approve or negative the motion which the consul, with the approval of the senate, laid before them. There was no discussion of any kind. The people were simply asked to say yes or no. Their power went no further, and there is no doubt that in most cases the vote of the people was a mere matter of form. When a question had been duly discussed in the senate and was, upon a decree of the senate, brought before the people by the executive magistrate, it would have been strange indeed and an ominous sign of internal dissensions, if the people had voted contrary to what was expected of them. In ordinary times the consul acted under the authority of the senate and the people under the authority of the consul, and thus the three apparently independent agents worked in harmony together because in reality one of them led and the others followed.

<small>Forms observed at the meetings of the comitia centuriata.</small>

We have now drawn such a sketch of the first republican constitution as our scanty sources justify. Meagre as it is, it enables us to form an opinion of its general character. It was a decidedly aristocratic form of government. The patricians were in possession of the executive power and of the priestly offices; they alone formed the senate, and they had such influence in the popular assembly of centuries that they were able to carry elections and resolutions in it in the patrician interest. But we cannot estimate the influence of these institutions on the nation at large, unless we can ascertain the proportion which the patricians bore to the whole Roman people as to wealth and numbers. If the governing body formed but a small nobility and nevertheless engrossed all political power, the constitution of the republic was in the highest degree unsafe and the position of the patricians quite untenable.

<small>Prevalence of patrician power in the state.</small>

for the physical strength represented by numbers is indispensable for the maintenance of the rule of one class over another. Unfortunately we have no data whatever to fix accurately the respective numbers of patricians and plebeians. In the beginning of the regal period, when the foundation of the state was laid, the patricians undoubtedly formed a people, or rather *the* people (the *populus Romanus*). They were the conquerors, who had won their position by force of arms. The conquered population, even if it had been more numerous, was not a match for them, and had to be content with toleration and protection. But it seems natural that a class which, like the patricians, received no addition from without, and which had to bear the brunt of all the numerous wars, must gradually have diminished in numbers, whereas the inferior citizens would be constantly recruited by the admission of conquered enemies and liberated slaves. Thus it would become imperatively necessary to strengthen the patrician combatants by plebeians, and this process found its legal expression in the establishment of the centuriate comitia. To be able to judge of the true character of the comitia centuriata we ought to know what proportion the plebeians bore in the centuries to the patricians. Did they form a considerable portion, or half, or more than half, or the whole of the 170 centuries of the infantry? Did the patricians form the 18 centuries of knights, or some of the centuries of the infantry, and how many? By putting these questions we have indicated already that the Roman historians leave us in doubt, and that we are driven to form our opinions independently of their evidence.

This is not the place to enumerate the various conjectures of writers, still less to discuss them. Perhaps we ought simply to confess our ignorance and our inability to supply the gap left by the silence of our informants. Still, without pretending to infallibility, we may venture to express an opinion, vague enough, yet better than mere vacuity. We think that when the centuriate assembly of the people was first established a body of plebeian companies was formed equal to that of the old patrician companies of fighting men. We think that the traces of this division of the whole people into two equal parts are discernible in the fact that the first class alone in the centuriate comitia contained 80 centuries, and the four succeeding classes only 90 centuries. The first class therefore was almost equal to all the others put together. If we take into consideration that the first class had originally the name of *classis* (*i.e.* army) to itself, and that the four other classes were designated as 'below the class' (*infra classem*), we can hardly fail to see that there must have been a difference of kind and not only of degree between the 80 centuries of the first class and the 90 centuries of the other classes. Now it is extremely probable that this difference was no other than the difference between patricians and plebeians, and that the reform which established the centuriate comitia consisted in this, that an equal number of plebeian companies (or centuries) was added to the existing number of patrician companies to form the army and the national assembly. This is the reform which, as we have several times hinted before, was effected in Rome by those military kings who succeeded the sacerdotal kings of the primeval period.

Probable origin of the comitia centuriata.

When the light of history begins to dawn upon the republic we find a state of things somewhat differing from this equal balance of patricians and plebeians in the army. It seems that the number of patricians must have greatly diminished, while that of the plebeians increased. The Roman armies are generally represented as essentially consisting of plebeians. Not so the political assembly of centuries. In this assembly the patricians for a long time had a decided majority; at least they were sufficiently strong in it to carry the elections in their own favour. This shows that the comitia centuriata, though originally the groundwork of the military organization, had come to be merely a political organization, and that the army was now formed on a different principle. That such was the case later in the history of Rome is well known; but what we do not know is the exact time when the separation took place between the political assembly and the army. In our opinion, this separation had taken place in that period of the republic which preceded the secession of the plebs; perhaps it was coeval with the establishment of the republic. For as it threw the great burden of military service chiefly upon the plebeians, whilst it reserved for the patricians the superiority in the voting assembly, it is in keeping with that aristocratic spirit which, as we have seen, characterized the republican revolution.

The assembly of centuries ceases to be military and becomes purely political.

The plebeians therefore found themselves in this position—that, whereas they were called upon to bear the burdens of citizenship and especially the greatest of them —viz., military service—they had little influence in the decisions of the sovereign assembly of citizens. Such a state of things could not last. It was overthrown by a great convulsion—the secession of the plebs, which might have led to the dissolution of the Roman commonwealth, but which, owing to the wise concessions of the senate and the patricians, laid the foundation of plebeian liberties.

CHAPTER XIII.

THE TRIBUNES OF THE PEOPLE.

ACCORDING to the account preserved by Livy and Dionysius, the patricians no sooner heard of the death of the exiled Tarquin than they began to oppress the plebeians, whom they had treated up to that time with great friendliness and leniency, in order to wean them from their attachment to the monarchy. Making use of the necessities of the impoverished commons, they lent them money on hard terms and relentlessly treated their insolvent debtors as slaves, loading them with fetters and driving their families from house and home. The plebeians could not bear the outrages of their oppressors any longer. They rose in a body, *Secession of the plebs.* left Rome, and encamped like a hostile army on a hill beyond the river Anio, at a distance of a few miles from the gates, with the intention of dissolving their connexion with their native city and of forming a separate community of their own. The patricians, unable to reduce them by force, and seeing that without the plebeians they were utterly helpless and exposed to foreign enemies, sent a message to the insurgents and entreated them to return. Both parties were inclined to a reconciliation. The plebeians asked for nothing but protection from the unjust treatment of patrician magistrates. It was stipulated that they should have the right to elect magistrates of their own, called tribunes of the plebs (*tribuni plebis*), empowered to act as their special patrons and protectors. They were to be invested with the right of 'intercession,' by which they could stop any legal or administrative proceedings directed against plebeians. This right of intercession, of which the patricians had already the benefit, inasmuch as either consul could use it against his colleague, was now extended to the plebeian tribunes, and afforded the same protection from arbitrary measures to a class of citizens which had hitherto been exposed without a remedy to illegal treatment. In order to give effect to the power of the tribunes, they were declared *sacrosancti, i.e.* inviolable. The curse of outlawry was pronounced against any man who should venture to resist or harm them. Upon these terms peace was concluded between the two orders of citizens, and the shedding of blood avoided; the covenant thus made was called a 'sacred law' (*lex sacrata*), and the hill on which the plebeians had encamped retained for all future ages the name of *Mons sacer*, the 'sacred hill.'

As no stipulations were made in the covenant about any remission of debts, nor the laws of debt altered, we may be sure that the cause which led to the secession was not a general indebtedness of the plebeians, as represented in the annals. It is indeed highly improbable that in the primitive state of society in which we must imagine the Romans then to have been, numerous loan transactions could have taken place. Moreover, as Sir G. C. Lewis remarks, 'it is difficult for us to conceive a state of society in which the poor are borrowers on a large scale.' To strengthen this impression of doubt we find that for a hundred years following the secession, *i.e.* up to the disasters of the Gallic conflagration, no further mention is made of any distress of the plebeians caused by debts; although, as already remarked, no remediary measures had been adopted. We may therefore feel sure that the cause of the secession was not the economic distress of the commons, but their exclusion from political rights, which left them without those safeguards from injustice which the patricians possessed.

The causes of the secession.

It is universally admitted that the original power of

the tribunes was the *jus auxilii*, or 'right of aid.' They could claim and did claim no more. They were far from usurping a share in the government of the republic. Their business was to protect plebeians from unjust treatment at the hands of patrician magistrates. From this humble origin they advanced by degrees to the power of controlling the whole civil government, and finally they became the instruments by means of which the republican constitution was changed into the empire.

Original power of the tribune.

At the same time with the tribuneship another plebeian office was established, that of ædiles, who were to act chiefly as the attendants and servants of the tribunes, and, like them, were invested with inviolability.

Plebeian ædiles.

The reason for investing the plebeian magistrates with the character of inviolability and of calling the laws that conferred this right 'sacred laws,' is to be found in the fact that from the patrician point of view the plebeians were looked upon as a distinct people, not fully and in every respect part of the *populus Romanus*. For this reason the agreement between the two parties was concluded in the form of an international treaty, with due observance of all those ceremonies—chiefly sacrifices and oaths—which were considered necessary when independent nations came to terms of amity. Oaths are an appeal not to a civil magistrate, but to a divine power,—the only power that can arbitrate between independent states. They are always employed to bind in their consciences those who cannot be compelled by a secular authority to fulfil their engagements. The patricians and the plebeians could not be looked upon as entirely members of one community as long as only the patricians had, through their auspices, intercourse with the gods of Rome, and for that reason excluded the plebeians

The sacred law.

from the government of the state; as long, also, as marriages between patricians and plebeians were unlawful. Therefore the magistrates of the plebs required to be specially protected by a sacred law, and, like the ambassadors of a foreign power, to be declared inviolable.

Antiquity of the tribuneship.

The ancient writers are unanimously of opinion that the offices of tribune and ædile were first created during the secession, and that they were in fact the fruit of that secession. But we may well ask if it is likely that the plebeians, who, as we have just seen, formed a separate community for themselves, had before that time no sort of organization of their own and no officers to regulate their affairs. It seems highly probable that the plebeians were not without such special plebeian magistrates, and if so, it seems most natural that these magistrates were no other than those tribunes and ædiles whom they chose as their legal patrons. The novelty introduced by the treaty of peace on the sacred hill consisted accordingly not in the creation of new offices, but in the solemn acknowledgment on the part of the patricians that the old plebeian magistrates should, under the guarantee of a *lex sacrata*, have authority to control the official acts even of patrician magistrates.

Control of the conscription by the tribunes.

What particular acts of patrician magistrates were likely to be specially obnoxious to plebeians we are not told; but it is not difficult to guess what they were. The principal burden of the citizens was the military service. The carrying on of the civil government entailed no expense. The Roman people did not groan under the weight of taxes. But every man was liable to be called out for military service, and it is clear that great injustice might be practised by the consuls if they disregarded the special claims of exemption which individual citizens might have. In such cases the tribunes would interfere, and their interference might amount to an inhibition of the whole conscription, so that they might actually veto a war if they were so minded. Their right in this respect resembled, therefore, the privilege of a popular chamber in modern times which refuses the supplies; and as this right has secured to modern parliaments the chief control of the state, so the *jus auxilii* of the tribunes contained the germ of their future power.

The number of tribunes originally chosen is stated variously to have been either two or five. This divergence of opinion is of little moment and affects only a very short period of time. All authors are agreed that from the Publilian law, passed in 471 B.C., *i.e.* 22 years after the first secession, the number was five, and was raised to ten in 457 B.C. Number of tribunes.

It is more annoying that doubts should exist with regard to the original mode of the election of the tribunes. Owing to the partly vague and partly contradictory statements of the writers on whom we depend for our information, the greatest difference of opinion prevails on this subject. We cannot here enter into a discussion of their conflicting statements, and it is therefore better at once to record the result to which a careful examination of the whole subject must lead us. It is this; that the tribunes of the plebs could have been elected neither by the patrician comitia curiata, nor by the military comitia centuriata, in which patricians and plebeians were mixed, but only by the comitia tributa,—the assembly of the plebeian tribes. What these comitia were we shall now proceed to inquire. Original mode of election.

The old patrician *populus*, as we have seen, was divided into tribes (the Ramnes, Tities, and Luceres), which were a division of the people, not of the territory. This division was the basis on which the comitia curiata were established (pp. 35, 108). The comitia curiata.

In the beginning of the republican period this division was superseded, and the division of the people into five classes was substituted, as we have seen, according to a property qualification. Thus arose the comitia centuriata. The five classes contained both patricians and plebeians. They were established in the first place for military, in the second, for political purposes. As an assembly for the election of the higher magistrates and for legislation, they continued in force to the end of the republic, but they ceased at an early period to be the basis on which the army was formed. The conscriptions for the army as far back as the light of history penetrates, were made not according to classes, but according to *tribes*, *i.e.* wards and districts, into which the town and territory were divided. These local tribes accordingly had nothing in common with the old patrician tribes but the name. Each tribe consisted of the Roman citizens settled within its boundaries, without regard either to descent or to property.

<small>Division of the land into local tribes.</small>

We are not informed when this division into tribes was first made. As long as the patricians had their own distinct organization (the old patrician tribes and curies), the division of the territory into local tribes would most probably affect the plebeians only, and whatever organization they had for self-government would be based on this division into local tribes. If they elected officers of their own, the forerunners of the famous tribunes of the plebs, these officers were of course elected by and for the tribes, whence they also derived their name. At some period which we cannot fix with accuracy, these tribes were made military districts, *i.e.* the troops were levied *tributim*, according to tribes. In fact, the whole administration of the republic was adjusted to this division of the territory, and when it became necessary to raise a *tribute*, or war-tax, for the expenses of a campaign, the tax was assessed *tributim*, according to tribes, from which circumstance it also received its name.

Thus arose a third form of popular assembly, the *comitia tributa*, or assembly of tribes. Being plebeian in its origin and representing that community of plebeians who, as we have seen, formed a distinct body in the Roman state and almost a separate people, apart from the patricians, the *comitia tributa* preserved this plebeian character throughout the whole history of the republic. Whereas the comitia curiata had been an aristocratic organization from which the plebeians were excluded, and the comitia centuriata had given a preponderance to wealth, the comitia tributa were purely democratic. They gave rich and poor an equal vote and excluded the patricians who were indeed unfit to assist in the transaction of the internal affairs of the plebeian body, and especially to take a share in the election of the tribunes of the plebs—officers whose chief duty it was to control the actions of patrician magistrates, and thus to be the special patrons of the plebeians. Plebeian character of the comitia tributa.

By the treaty on the Mons Sacer, the comitia of tribes—*i.e.* the plebeian assemblies of citizens—were first recognized by the patricians as invested with political rights, for the patricians bound themselves to treat the tribunes of the plebs elected in those comitia as persons invested with public authority. They could no longer ignore the public and official character of the tribunes, which we may suppose might have been their practice before the secession. The comitia of the plebs, therefore, from this moment acquired rights co-extensive with the rights of the comitia of centuries, though exerted in a different direction. If the centuries continued to elect the consuls, the tribes now elected tribunes and ædiles, and the The comitia tributa recognized as a sovereign assembly.

authority of these officers was acknowledged by the whole community. By-and-by, as we shall see, the comitia of tribes extended their sphere of action, whilst the centuries remained stationary. The comitia of tribes under the direction of the tribunes of the plebs became the moving power in the commonwealth to which all progress in constitutional and civil law is chiefly due. The comitia of centuries merely retained the privileges which they already possessed, viz. the election of consuls (and afterwards of prætors and censors, which offices had branched off from the consulship), the right to declare war, the decision in criminal appeals, and the legislation in constitutional law.

The original number of local tribes was twenty; four of them were city wards, the remaining sixteen country districts. Soon after the establishment of the republic a new tribe was added, and their number thus raised to twenty-one; this number of tribes remained stationary for upwards of one hundred years. Then began the career of conquest. New tribes were formed out of the territory acquired in Etruria, Latium, and in the land of the Aequians and Volscians, until in 241 B.C. the number thirty-five was reached, and the Roman citizens had become so numerous and lived at such great distances from one another that meetings in Rome for legislation and election had become physically impossible to the mass of them. Nevertheless, the Romans, with their spirit of conservatism, retained the comitia tributa to the end of the republic, when they were swept away with the general wreck of the old worn-out and antiquated institutions.

<small>Number of local tribes.</small>

CHAPTER XIV.

THE AGRARIAN LAW OF SPURIUS CASSIUS.

THE great disparity of political rights which separated patricians and plebeians had its counterpart in the economic relations of the two classes of citizens. The patricians are always represented as the rich, the plebeians as the poor. In a rude age, when the industrial arts and trade were all but unknown, wealth consisted chiefly in the possession of land and cattle. The Latin tongue, by calling money *pecunia*, *i.e.* 'cattle' (chattels), sufficiently denotes this original identity of wealth with land and the produce of land. That the patricians, as the wealthy, were the chief owners of the soil, we might infer *à priori* from the circumstance of their being the governing class and the original conquerors of the land; for it was the invariable practice in ancient Italy (a practice followed by the Romans themselves in historical times) for the conquerors to treat the conquered land as forfeited, and to make such new dispositions with regard to it as suited their purposes. They usually left only a portion of it, one half or even less, to the old owners, and took the remainder for themselves. This was declared public land, *i.e.* the land of the *populus* or governing people, and was occupied by members of the ruling body, who used either to cultivate it themselves or give it in lots to be held and cultivated by their dependents or clients. None of this land reserved for the populus could be occupied by the inferior class of citizens, nor could such portions of it as were left in pasture be used by them. Other restrictions may be supposed to have been made; for instance, the prohibition of the free purchase or inheritance of land which had been set apart for the ruling class.

[margin: Wealth and poverty.]

[margin: Disposal of conquered land.]

As long as the memory of conquest was fresh in men's minds, such institutions would not be felt to involve cruelty or hardship; for, according to the law of ancient warfare, not only the property, but even the liberty and life of a conquered people were at the mercy of their conquerors. Whatever was left to them was a free gift, and would be appreciated as such. But when in course of time the two classes had gradually grown into one people, it would be felt that the traces of the original wrong inflicted by the stronger ought to be effaced. As demands were made by the plebeians for civil rights, so they naturally began to claim a release from those restrictions under which they had hitherto lain with regard to the tenure and enjoyment of land.

Rise of discontent among the plebeians.

This is the origin and meaning of the agrarian laws which agitated the early republic side by side with the contests about political rights. They did not and could not refer to the disposal of newly-conquered land; for at the time when we hear of the first agrarian disputes there were no new conquests made by Rome and therefore there was no land to distribute. At a later period the case was different. When Rome entered on her career of conquest, and large tracts of public land were at her disposal, the agrarian disputes referred to these new acquisitions and had consequently an entirely different character.

The agrarian laws.

The first agrarian law is said to have been proposed by a patrician, Spurius Cassius, who was consul in the year of the secession, 493 B.C., and again seven years later. The descriptions of his proposals given by our informants are so confused and palpably erroneous that we can make nothing of them. They proceed on the false assumption that Rome had a great deal of conquered land to distribute,

The proposals of Spurius Cassius.

and they mix up the account of the agrarian law with the conditions of a league said to have been concluded at the same time between Rome and her neighbours, the Latins and the Hernicans. We cannot attempt here to unravel the errors into which the annalists have fallen, nor to discuss the different opinions held about the nature of the agrarian law of Cassius. We confine ourselves to pointing out the apparent connexion of this proposal with the struggles of the plebeians for more equal rights, which seems to be evident from the facts that Spurius Cassius was consul in the year of the secession and that he brought forward his motion in his next consulship. He was the first patrician who espoused the cause of the plebeians, and the first also who paid the price of such a policy. He was charged with treasonable designs, and condemned to death; his law was not carried into effect. It remained a dead letter, though it acted as a stimulus to continued agitation.

CHAPTER XV.

THE LEAGUE WITH THE LATINS AND HERNICANS.

THE principle of confederation, which was the chief cause of Roman greatness, seems to have been common to all the aboriginal races of Italy, and, in fact, was forced upon them by the necessities of their situation. In a time of almost inces-sant warfare an isolated community would soon have been the prey of some powerful foe, if it had not sought security in an alliance with neighbouring cities equally in want of assistance. Thus arose the old league of the Latins, of which in pre-historic times Alba Longa was the head,

Prevalence of confederations.

and the temple of Jupiter Latiaris on the Alban mount, the common sanctuary. We do not know when and how this league was dissolved and Alba destroyed: for the story of her destruction by the third king of Rome is in every respect legendary.

Yet there is no reason to doubt that Rome, as reported, succeeded Alba in the headship of Latium. We hear of no other power strong enough to have brought about the downfall of that city; and Rome was always looked upon as the successor of Alba, and took the presidency at the annual festival of the Latins on the Alban mount. The stories of the later kings represent Rome as ruling over the Latins. Under Servius Tullius it is said that a temple of Diana was built on the Aventine hill as a common sanctuary of the Latins and the Romans. The younger Tarquin, we are told, reduced the towns of Latium by force and fraud, and extended his dominion over the whole country. Whatever may be the truth of these stories, the supremacy of Rome over Latium, if it really existed towards the close of the regal period, came to an end with the expulsion of the kings. In all probability, as we have seen above, the Latins helped the Romans to throw off the common yoke, and both Latins and Romans became free at the same time.

<small>Rome the head of a pre-historic league.</small>

The pretended victory of Rome over the combined cities of Latium, at Lake Regillus, is a fable or a misrepresentation. (*See* p. 80.) The Latins were so far from being conquered by republican Rome, that the same year—493 B.C.—which witnessed the secession of the plebs and the establishment of the plebeian tribunate, is marked by the conclusion of a treaty between Rome and Latium, in which both appear as independent powers.

<small>New league between Rome and Latium.</small>

That such a treaty was concluded is certain, for it

lasted for more than a century and a half—that is to say, down to a period in which the leading events are no longer subject to historical doubts. Nor is it difficult to understand the motives which induced the two nations to conclude such an alliance. It was a renewal of that old union between the two kindred races, which appears to have been temporarily dissolved after the Roman revolution, and it was dictated by the common interests of both. The war with the Tarquins and the Etruscans, as we have surmised, was a common war of liberation; and the Etruscans remained for many years the common enemies of Rome and Latium. Other aggressors threatened both nations in the east and south. In the east the Aequians, a hardy and rapacious tribe of mountaineers, and in the south the warlike Volscians, were pressing upon them. The Latin towns formed for Rome a line of fortifications on the south and east against these assaults, and Rome defended for Latium the line of the Tiber against the Etruscans on the western and northern sides. Thus both peoples were largely benefited by a league for mutual protection, and it seems to be hardly doubtful that the preservation of the independence as well of Latium as of Rome is due chiefly to this wise policy.

Motives for concluding the league.

The league between Rome and Latium is said to have been concluded by Spurius Cassius, who was consul in the year 493 B.C., and author of the agrarian law in his third consulship, 486 B.C. Soon afterwards another nation, the Hernicans, who lived further eastward between the Aequians and the Volscians, joined the league on equal terms. The object of the league being simply mutual protection in war, it left the independence of each contracting city unimpaired. But it is in the nature of such alliances that the stronger members gradually acquire an ascendency which is very nearly

Object and effect of the league.

akin to dominion. Rome, by virtue of her extent and population, was by far the most powerful and consequently the leading member of the league. In course of time some of the Latin towns fell into decay owing to the ravages of the Aequians and Volscians; others were actually destroyed and laid waste; others fell into the hands of the enemies and became Aequian or Volscian towns in Latium. Rome and her allies were by no means always victorious. On the contrary, for more than a hundred years they suffered more harm than they inflicted. The Volscians succeeded in penetrating into the very heart of Latium, threatening even Rome itself. The Aequians lay like a hostile garrison on Mount Algidus in the immediate vicinity of Tibur and Praeneste. War raged from year to year. Military training was more important than peaceful work. The Roman citizens and their Latin allies acquired in this hard school that discipline and warlike spirit, that unshaken bravery and endurance which distinguished them ever after. Whatever the hardships and miseries of this period were, the walls of Rome resisted all attacks, whilst the Latins suffered so much that they were reduced from the rank of allies to that of subjects. The league thus proved highly beneficial to Rome. It served to protect her, and it raised her to a pre-eminence which she could not have otherwise attained.

CHAPTER XVI.

THE WARS WITH THE VOLSCIANS AND AEQUIANS.

THE history of the wars with the Volscians and Aequians, as narrated by Livy, is destitute of all historical value. It is a succession of battles, sieges, triumphs and reverses, which are evidently the product of the imagination, with a very slight infusion of trustworthy tradition. Exaggeration, vainglory and repetition, reckless invention and contradiction are discoverable on every page. It would be in the highest degree unprofitable to examine these accounts in detail, and to burthen the memory with facts, dates, and names so unreal. We shall content ourselves with justifying this opinion by reviewing shortly the celebrated stories of Coriolanus and Cincinnatus, as characteristic both of the wars to which they refer and of the historians who relate them.

In the year after the secession of the plebs (492 B.C.) there was a famine in Rome; for during the civil contention the plebeians had not cultivated their own lands, and they had laid waste the fields of their adversaries. There was, therefore, great distress among the poor plebeians, and they would have fallen victims to hunger if the consuls had not bought corn in Etruria and distributed it to the starving people. But even this was not sufficient, and the people suffered great want, till corn arrived from Sicily, which Dionysius, the tyrant of Syracuse, sent as a present to the Romans.

The story of Coriolanus.

There was at that time in Rome a brave patrician, whose name was Caius Marcius. He had conquered the town of Corioli in the preceding year when the Romans were carrying on war with the Volscians, and for this reason his fellow-soldiers had given him the surname Coriolanus. This man set himself stoutly against the plebeians, for he hated them because they had won the tribuneship from the senate. He therefore advised the consuls not to divide the corn among the plebeians unless they surrendered their newly-acquired right and abolished the office of the tribunes.

When the plebeians heard this they were enraged, and would have killed him had not the tribunes protected him from the fury of the crowd, and accused him before the assembly of the people of having broken the peace and violated the sacred laws. But Coriolanus mocked the people and the tribunes, showing haughty defiance and presumptuous pride; and as he did not appear before the people assembled to try him, he was banished. Vowing that he would be revenged on his enemies, he went to Antium, where he lived as the guest of Attius Tullius, the chief of the Volscians. After this the two men consulted together how they might persuade the Volscians to make war on the Romans. It happened that at this time the great games were celebrated in Rome in honour of Jupiter; and a great number of Volscians came to Rome to see the games. Then Attius Tullius went secretly to the consuls, and advised them to take care that his countrymen did not break the peace during the festive season. When the consuls heard this, they sent heralds through the town, and caused it to be proclaimed that all the Volscians should leave the town before night. The Volscians, exasperated at this outrage to their nation, proceeded in a body to return home by the Latin road. This road led past the spring of Ferentina, where at one time the Latins used to hold their councils. Here Attius was waiting for his countrymen, and excited them against Rome, saying that they had been shut out unjustly from sharing in the sacred festivities, as if they had been guilty of sacrilege, or were not worthy to be treated as allies and friends by the Roman people. Thus a new war with Rome was decided on, and Attius Tullius and C. Marcius Coriolanus set out with a large army, and conquered in one campaign many of the most important towns of Latium.

After this the Volscians advanced to Rome, and encamping near the Fossa Cluilia, five miles from the town, they laid waste the lands of the plebeians round about. Then the Romans were seized with despair, and were afraid to advance against the Volscians or fight them in the field; but looking for deliverance only from the mercy of their conquerors, they sent the principal senators as ambassadors to Coriolanus to sue for peace But Coriolanus answered that, unless the Romans restored to the Volscians all the conquered towns, peace would not be granted. When the same ambassadors came a second time to ask for more favourable conditions, Coriolanus would not even see them. Thereupon the chief priests came to his tent in their sacred robes and with the insignia of their office, and tried to calm his anger. But they strove in vain. At last the noblest Roman matrons came to Veturia, the mother of Coriolanus, and to Volumnia, his wife, and persuaded them to accompany them into the enemy's camp, and with their prayers and tears to soften the conqueror's heart and to save the town, which the men could not protect with their arms.

Now, when the procession of Roman matrons approached the Volscian camp, and Coriolanus recognized his mother, his wife, and his little children, he was deeply moved, and listened to the entreaties of the matrons, and granted their request, saying, 'O, my mother! Rome thou hast saved, but thou hast lost thy son.' And forthwith he led the army of the Volscians away from Rome, and gave back all the conquered towns. But he never returned to Rome, because he had been banished by the people, and he closed his life in exile among the Volscians.

The whole of this pretty story when examined by the light of historical criticism vanishes into air. Neither the hero's name, nor his banishment, nor his rapid conquests, nor the intercession of the Roman matrons, belong to history. We know for certain that Scipio Africanus, more than 400 years later, was the first Roman who received a surname to

Criticism of the story of Coriolanus.

commemorate a conquest. Hence Caius Marcius could not have been called Coriolanus from the capture of Corioli. Besides, Corioli could hardly have been taken by the Romans from the Volscians in 492, as in 493 it is enumerated among the Latin cities which concluded a league with Rome. The Volscians, the constant enemies of the republic, could not be present at the Roman games, nor could they assemble at the grove of Ferentina, which was a trysting-place of the Latins. Coriolanus could not be banished by the Roman plebeians on the accusation of the tribunes, for the tribunes who had just been elected had as yet only the right of protecting plebeians from unjust treatment, not the power of prosecuting patricians before an assembly of the plebs. The rapid conquests of the Volscians under the command of Coriolanus are nothing short of miraculous. The capture of twelve towns in one summer campaign is a success which suits fiction, but is unequalled in the history of early Rome. Yet after such conquests Coriolanus insists upon the Romans giving up these towns, as if he could not hold what he had taken; and when he is induced by private and personal motives to make peace, he is so reckless of the interests of his Volscian friends, who after all were the real conquerors, that he generously restores his conquests to the Romans. These Romans, at other times so ready to come forward and fight their enemies, shrink like cowards behind their walls and send messages to entreat the mercy of the conqueror, without, however, offering the slightest concessions. They hit upon a novel scheme. They send priests to propitiate the anger of their exasperated fellow-citizen, a thing which they never did before or after, and which their whole system of public and sacred law forbade. More than that, an embassy of matrons comes out to the hostile camp. We almost fancy we see again the Sabine matrons who rushed between the angry combatants to establish peace in the time of Romulus. Such a scene is effective and proper in fiction, but impossible in the history of Rome. Neither matrons nor priests could be employed on political embassies. The writer who invented such a story must have been ignorant of Roman institutions.

What circumstance gave rise to the story of Coriolanus it is impossible for us to say. It may be a mere fiction designed to glorify the Roman matrons. At any rate, it was not calculated to throw light on the history of the Volscian wars. *Effect of the Volscian wars.* These wars continued, apparently without interruption, during the whole period we have under review. The Volscians obtained a settlement in southern Latium, where their most important town was the seaport, Antium. But after the decemvirate (450 B.C.) their power visibly decreased. The Romans and Latins recovered some of the lost ground, and finally extended their league over the whole district from the Tiber to the confines of Campania.

Peace was concluded with the Aequians in the year 459 B.C., and the Romans expected no hostilities on that side. But soon after this the faithless Aequians suddenly invaded the country of Tusculum, and their commander, Gracchus Cloelius, *The story of Cincinnatus.* pitched his camp on the hill Algidus, the eastern spur of the Alban range, from whence he laid waste the land of the Roman allies. Here Quintus Fabius appeared before him at the head of an embassy, and demanded satisfaction and compensation. But Cloelius laughed at the ambassadors, and, mocking them, said they should lay their complaints before the oak tree under which his tent was pitched. Then the Romans took the oak and all the gods to witness that the Aequians had broken the peace and had begun an unrighteous war; and without delay the consul Minucius led an army against them. But the chances of war were not in his favour. He was defeated, and blockaded in his camp. At this news terror prevailed in Rome as if the enemy were at the very gates; for the second consul was far away with his army, fighting with the Sabines, the allies of the Aequians.

There was nothing now to be done but to name a dictator, and only one man seemed to be fit to fill the post. This was Lucius Quinctius Cincinnatus, a noble patrician who had long served his country in peace and war as senator and consul, and was then living quietly at home cultivating his small estate with his own hands. Now, when the messengers of the senate came to Cincinnatus to announce to him that he was nominated dictator, they found him ploughing, and he had taken off his garments, for the heat was great. Therefore he first asked his wife to bring him his toga, that he might receive the message of the senate in a becoming manner. And when he had heard their errand, he went with them into the town, accepted the dictatorship, and chose for the master of the horse Lucius Tarquitius, a noble but poor patrician. Then, having ordered that all the courts of justice should be closed, and all common business suspended till the danger was averted from the country, he summoned all men who could bear arms to meet in the evening on the Field of Mars, every man with twelve stakes for ramparts, and provisions for five days; and before the sun went down the army had started off, and reached Mount Algidus at midnight.

Now, when the dictator saw that they were drawing near to the enemy, he bade the men halt and throw their baggage in a heap, and he quietly surrounded the camp of the Aequians, and gave orders to make a ditch round the enemy and drive in the stakes. Then the Romans raised a loud cry, so that the Aequians were overcome by terror and despair; but the legions of the consul Minucius recognized the war-cry of their countrymen, seized their arms, and sallied forth from their camp. Thus the Aequians were attacked on both sides, and seeing there was no escape, surrendered, and prayed for mercy. Cincinnatus granted them their lives, and allowed them all to depart home unharmed after passing naked under the yoke, except Gracchus Cloelius and the other commanders. These he kept as prisoners of war, and he divided the spoil among his victorious soldiers. In this manner Cincinnatus rescued the blockaded army, and returned in triumph to Rome; and when he had delivered his country from its enemies, he laid down his office on the sixteenth day, and returned to his fields, crowned with glory and honoured by the people, but poor, and contented in his poverty.

The story of Cincinnatus differs in character from that of Coriolanus, and seems to have a genuine historical basis. It is not a mere fiction, but only a boastful, distorted, and exaggerated account of what may have really happened, and it is in so far a good specimen of the usual performances of the Roman annalists. It is also worthy of notice that with some variations it is related not less than five times under five different years (466, 460, 458, 443, 440 B.C.). It cannot, therefore, contribute much to our knowledge of the wars with the Aequians. Exaggerations of the story.

These wars continued to harass Rome and her allies for the whole of the first century of the republic, and, like the Volscian wars, contributed to enforce military discipline upon the citizens and to improve their tactics, whilst the constantly impending danger arising from them had no doubt the effect of mitigating the internal conflicts between patricians and plebeians. For nearly fifty years the Character of the Aequian wars.

Romans and their allies were hard pressed. The Aequians established themselves on the Alban hills in the heart of Latium, whence they pushed their inroads to the very walls of Rome. But it seems that after the decemvirate the Aequians, like the Volscians, relaxed in their national vigour. Whether owing to the hostility of the Samnites in their rear, or to other causes, they gradually ceased to be dangerous, so that the Romans were enabled to turn their attention to the north-west and to begin their career of conquest on the side of Etruria.

CHAPTER XVII.

WAR WITH THE ETRUSCANS.

WHEN, in the beginning of the republic, the Etruscans were expelled from Latium, they did not entirely lose their hold of the country on that side of the Tiber. They continued masters of Fidenae, a strong town at a distance of but five miles from Rome. Constant hostilities seem to have gone on between the Romans and the people of Fidenae, in which the latter were usually supported by their countrymen across the Tiber, especially the Veientines. In fact, Fidenae, at an equal distance from Rome and Veii, seems to have been a military post of the latter town, a *tête de pont* on the left bank of the Tiber, by which the Veientines were enabled, whenever they liked, to cross the river into Latium and to harass Rome and her allies by their plundering incursions.

The Etruscan town of Fidenae.

It was obviously to obtain a similar footing on the Etruscan side of the Tiber that in 479 B.C. the Romans determined to establish a fort on the small river Cremera not far from Veii. Such military settlements were a characteristic feature

Roman fort on the Cremera.

of the early wars in Italy as well as Greece, as they enabled invaders to secure their hold on conquered districts. The colonies which Rome established in the course of her conquests were mainly such military posts, and proved the successful means of incorporating gradually the whole peninsula in the dominion of the republic.

The settlement on the Cremera gave rise to a popular legend not less characteristic of the early wars and of the style of the early annals than the stories of Coriolanus and Cincinnatus. The noble house of the Fabii, it is said, volunteered to secure Rome from the inroads of the Veientines. They obtained the sanction of the senate for this patriotic enterprise, mustered the whole strength of the house, 306 fighting men, and marched out under the command of Kaeso Fabius, the consul, to carry on the war with Veii at their own risk and expense. They built a fort on the river Cremera in the neighbourhood of Veii, and sallying forth from this place of safety, they ravaged the land of the Veientines and kept them in check for two years, so that they could not think of carrying the war across the Tiber. But when, on the anniversary of a solemn festival of their family, the Fabii proceeded in peaceful guise to offer up a sacrifice on the Quirinal hill, the Veientines, disregarding the truce of the gods, laid an ambush on the road to Rome, fell upon the Fabii unawares, and killed them to a man. Thus the whole Fabian house would have been extirpated, had not one boy been left behind at Rome, on account of his tender age, when the men of his house marched out to fight the Veientines. This child became the ancestor of the Fabii, who served the state for many years as men eminent in council and in the field.

Story of the Fabii.

The disasters of the Fabii almost proved fatal to Rome.

The Veientines, following up their success, defeated a Roman army under the consul Menenius, and actually effected a lodgment on the hill Janiculus opposite Rome. They crossed the Tiber and cut off Rome from Latium. But the size and natural strength of the capital proved the safety of the republic. The Veientines, unable to carry on a regular siege, were beaten off in a series of engagements, driven from the Janiculus, and compelled to seek a refuge in their own country. The war ended in an armistice for forty years, and Rome was thus enabled to direct all her strength against her inveterate enemies on the east and south.

There is no reason to doubt that the legend of the Fabii on the Cremera has a foundation in fact. It was recorded, probably in the pontifical annals, that on their march to that fatal expedition the 306 men went through the right-hand arch of the Porta Carmentalis, and this passage was for ever after held to be unlucky, and was avoided by soldiers leaving the city for the field. But we must, of course, expect to find the story decked out with fictitious ornaments, and disfigured, as is usual in the early annals of Rome, by exaggerations and inconsistencies. We can discover in it, we think, the spirit of a Fabian family chronicler who drew his information from funeral orations of the Fabian house. It all redounds to the glory of this great family. The Fabii wage war for the republic on their own account. They number 306 fighting men, a figure palpably and foolishly exaggerated. And to make the story more telling, the narrator informs us that in this large house there was just one child of an age so tender that he could not join the expedition, and thus was left behind. It is not necessary to point out the physical impossibility of a proportion of one boy to 306

Historical foundation of the story.

men. Vagaries of fancy such as this we must take into the bargain, and rest thankful if the story is not altogether devoid of all elements of historical truth.

The peace or truce concluded between Rome and Veii in 474 B.C. seems to have been observed faithfully on both sides. We hear of no hostilities between the two nations till 438 B.C., when the wars began which finally led to the destruction of the Etruscan city in 396 B.C.

CHAPTER XVIII.

THE DECEMVIRS AND THE LAWS OF THE TWELVE TABLES.—451-442 B.C.

By the establishment of the office of tribunes, 493 B.C., the plebeian assembly of tribes acquired the rank and weight of a national assembly, inasmuch as the officers elected by it were invested with public authority, and were recognized and submitted to by the patricians no less than the plebeians. It seems that in consequence of the extended rights thus gained by the comitia of tribes the patricians claimed to have votes in them. If they had succeeded in this claim, the tribunes would have ceased to be magistrates of the plebs alone; they would have become, what the consuls were, viz., magistrates not of a class or fraction of the Roman people, but of the whole community; patricians would have become eligible to the office, and the great contrast between patricians and plebeians would have gradually disappeared. Perhaps this would have been salutary in the end. But the plebeians vehemently opposed the admission of patricians into their own comitia. They would not allow their patrons, the tribunes, to be elected by anybody but themselves, and they insisted upon the

The Publilian law.

rigid exclusion of patricians from the plebeian assembly. A law was passed in 471 B.C., called, after its author, **Volero** Publilius, the Publilian law, to secure the election of the plebeian tribunes exclusively to the plebs.

This law, passed only twenty-two years after the secession, did not introduce a new principle but was only declaratory of an established right. By it, moreover, according to some writers, the number of tribunes was raised from two to five.

The tribunes of the people did not long confine themselves to the duties for which they were primarily elected.

<small>Advancing claims of the plebeians.</small> Not satisfied with protecting plebeians from unjust treatment of patrician magistrates, they aimed at raising the inferior citizens to an equality with the ruling class in all private and public rights. The times were past when the patricians could claim to represent the people of Rome and to wield exclusively all political power. It had become clear on the occasion of the secession that the patricians were helpless without the plebeians. The frequent wars could not be carried on without the men, who by that time undoubtedly formed the greater part of the army. The privileges of birth, of presumed sanctity, of exclusive political and legal experience, and, above all, of prescriptive possession of power, could not outweigh the claim which the plebeians now put forth as the great bulk of the people and especially of the fighting men.

The first object of the plebeians, however, was not a share of political power, but a more effective legal pro-

<small>The Terentilian Rogations.</small> tection than even the new office of tribunes had secured for them. They asked for two things—first, the removal of all inequalities between themselves and the patricians as far as private rights were concerned; and, secondly, a codification of

the laws thus reformed. This was the object of an agitation set on foot by Terentilius Arsa, a tribune of the people, in 462 B.C.

The motion of Terentilius met with a violent opposition from those conservative politicians who felt and acted as if human institutions ought to be unchangeable, like the laws of nature. The contest lasted for ten years. The tribunes had as yet no seats in the senate, and were therefore unable to advocate their projected reform in that assembly. They could only harangue their fellow plebeians in public meetings, called 'contiones'; but these contiones had not, like the comitia, the power of passing laws. The agitation of the tribunes therefore resembled that which is exercised in modern times by the press or by public meetings. To obtain the force of law, like an act of parliament, the proposals of the tribunes had to be sanctioned by a majority of the senators; and this was exceedingly difficult to effect at a time when the senate consisted as yet entirely of patricians and did not admit the tribunes of the plebs to a seat or a vote. There would have been no prospect of final success if the senators had to a man resisted the reform. But fortunately for Rome the ruling class did not consist exclusively of men opposed to all progress. Like the English nobility, it seems to have included at all times a number of men enlightened enough to see that reforms are sometimes demanded by the necessities of national life, if not by generosity or justice. Such were the Valerii, Spurius Cassius, M. Manlius, and, above all, the members of the Claudian family—men of a haughty and overbearing spirit, yet ready to encounter the hostility of the ruling class for the benefit of the greater number and of the state. These men had the wisdom to see that Rome had no chance of making head against

The Claudian family.

her numerous enemies all around, if she was paralysed by discord and civil strife at home. They counselled conciliation, which had been found effective on the occasion of the secession thirty years before; and it was owing to their exertions, no doubt, that several concessions were made to the plebeians, such as the increase of the number of tribunes from five to ten, the limitation of the fines which magistrates should be allowed to inflict, and a change in the tenure of land on the Aventine hill in favour of the plebs (the law of Icilius 'de Aventino publicando'), the exact nature of which we are unfortunately unable to understand.

<small>Concessions to the plebs.</small>

Yet these concessions, if they were intended to make the plebeians forego the desire of the reform of Terentilius, proved of no effect. Year after year the demand for law reform was repeated; and at last, after a struggle, protracted through ten years, the government, *i.e.* the senate, in the name of the patrician body, consented. It was agreed that the existing forms of government should be suspended; that in the place of the patrician consuls and the plebeian tribunes ten men, 'decemvirs,' should be elected indiscriminately from the two orders of citizens, empowered to carry on the regular government, and at the same time to reform the existing law, and to equalise the private rights of plebeians and patricians; finally, in order to prevent any ambiguity, and to put an end to the uncertainty inseparable from unwritten laws, it was resolved that the laws should be written down and made known to the public.

<small>Election of decemvirs.</small>

The laws of the Twelve Tables, drawn up in consequence of this resolution, continued in force for many ages, and even in Cicero's time formed part of the elementary school teaching of Roman boys. Unfortunately, only fragments of them have come down to us. Yet these fragments are of invaluable

<small>The laws of the Twelve Tables.</small>

service in the study of Roman life and manners. The documentary history of Rome may be said to begin with these laws.

The time of legendary stories and of mere tradition is past. Nevertheless when we read the account given by Livy of the transactions which led to the legislation of the decemvirs and especially of those which caused their overthrow, we feel the greatest disappointment and irritation; for instead of a plain, unvarnished tale we find statements so contradictory, unintelligible, and incredible that we cannot possibly accept them as they are, although we have not sufficient external evidence to sift and to correct them. We can only hope to test them by general arguments and by applying to them the laws of historical probability, availing ourselves at the same time of some features of the story, which we have a right to look upon as remnants of a trustworthy tradition. *Perplexities of the annalistic accounts.*

Before the decemvirs entered on their office, it was determined, as Livy informs us, to send an embassy to Athens for the purpose of studying the celebrated laws of Solon, that the Roman legislators might be enabled to form their laws after that great model. The names of the three ambassadors are given by Livy, as well as that of a Greek philosopher who accompanied them and assisted them in their task. Upon their return they made their report, and the services of the Greek philosopher were rated so high that a statue was erected in his honour in the Roman Forum. *Embassy to Athens.*

In spite of the apparent evidence which may seem to be contained in the erection of this statue, we can have no hesitation in declaring the whole story of the Greek embassy a fiction, for the following reasons :

No nation of antiquity every dreamt of forming its

civil law after a foreign model. Least of all would the Romans have done so, who, if they were original in anything, were original in their system of civil law and distinguished by their contempt for foreign institutions.

If this were not so, we should be able to discover some such resemblance between the Solonian and Roman laws as would be evidence of the derivation of the latter from the former. No such resemblance exists. Nor is it possible to conceive that Roman ambassadors could have gone to Athens to study the laws of Solon, for at the time of the decemvirs these laws were no longer in force, but had been supplanted by the democratic institutions of Kleisthenes. Apart from the reasons just urged, the Romans at the period of the decemvirs, in the middle of the fifth century before Christ, if they had ever heard the name of Solon or of Athens, were probably very far from such a general acquaintance with Greece as is implied by a resolution to take Greek models for their own national legislation. We cannot do better than sum up these doubts in the words of Gibbon: 'From a motive of national pride both Livy and Dionysius are willing to believe that the deputies of Rome visited Athens under the wise and splendid administration of Pericles, and the laws of Solon were transfused into the Twelve Tables. If such an embassy had indeed been received from the barbarians of Hesperia, the Roman name would have been familiar to the Greeks before the reign of Alexander, and the faintest evidence would have been explored and celebrated by the curiosity of succeeding times. But the Athenian monuments are silent; nor will it seem credible that the patricians should undertake a long and perilous navigation to copy the purest model of a democracy. In the comparison of the tables of Solon with

Reasons for rejecting this story.

those of the decemvirs some casual resemblance may be found—some rules which nature and reason have revealed to every society. But in all the great lines of public and private jurisprudence the legislators of Rome and Athens appear to be strangers or adverse to each other.'

Having disposed of the story of the Athenian embassy, we proceed to examine the narrative of the decemviral legislation.

In 451 B.C. the elections of decemvirs took place, and resulted in the return of ten patricians. The plebeians being left without their tribunes had to submit to this violation of the recent agreement, which stipulated for a mixed commission. However, the patrician decemvirs discharged their duties honestly and almost completed their task, so that before the end of the year ten tables of the laws were drawn up and approved by the people. *The traditional story of the decemvirs.*

As some laws were still wanting to complete the code, it was resolved that decemvirs should again be elected for the following year. Then Appius Claudius, who had been the leading man in the first year's commission, and who was looked upon as the champion of the aristocratic party, suddenly assumed, it is said, the character of a friend of the people, and secured not only his own re-election but also the election of several plebeians upon the new commission. However, when he and his colleagues were installed in office they showed that they were the friends neither of the patricians nor of the plebeians, for they treated both with equal violence. They appeared in public, preceded by a body of 120 lictors, and these lictors carried not only the rods, but also the axes, the emblems of dictatorial power. All freedom was suppressed; no class of citizens was spared. Not only were the plebeians trampled under foot, but the most eminent of the patricians were put to death or driven into banishment. Rome was like a city taken by storm and sacked by a victorious enemy.

Thus the year of the second decemvirate passed by, and yet the two tables which were wanted to complete the legislation were not submitted to the people for approbation. The decemvirs refused to lay down their office, protesting that they would first pass the laws which they were appointed to draw up. The senate in vain urged them to retire; the people became discontented, the army mutinous; yet the decemvirs clung to their office, thus violating the fundamental law of the republic, which required every magistrate to resign at the expiration of the period for which he was elected.

The general disaffection was brought to a crisis by an outrage committed on female chastity by Appius Claudius himself. In the blindness of his passion for a beautiful girl, the daughter of Virginius, a brave plebeian centurion, he instigated one of his clients to claim her as his slave, under the pretext that she was the daughter of a slave woman belonging to him. The girl was brought before the judgment seat of Appius, and he, contrary to a clear provision of the law sanctioned by himself, decided that pending the investigation she should be considered not as a free woman, but as a slave, and handed over to the keeping of the claimant. With difficulty the friends of Virginia obtained a respite for her, until her father should appear, to produce the evidence in favour of his daughter's legitimate birth. On the following day the case was proceeded with; and when Virginius saw that all his arguments and entreaties were of no avail to save his child from shame, he stabbed her to death with his own hand.

This deed was the signal for a general insurrection. The people, a second time in arms, seceded to the Sacred

Mount, threatening to abandon Rome and to form a separate community. The senate and the patricians, left behind in Rome, at last compelled the decemvirs to resign, and then restored the consular government. Thus they induced the commons to return after the re-enactment of the sacred laws and the re-establishment of the tribuneship. The decemvirs were punished with exile. Appius Claudius, reserved in prison for a severer punishment, put an end to his own life.

Thus runs the wonderful story of the downfall of the decemvirs. It is hardly necessary to say that it cannot be true. The sudden change in the character of Appius Claudius, however strange, is perhaps possible; but what shall we think of the policy ascribed to the decemvirs, which was hostile to both parties in the state at once, and seems to have rested on no support save that of their 120 lictors? Surely the Roman plebs, united in common interests with the patricians, were not obliged to have recourse to such a violent measure as a secession in order to get rid of a few magistrates. That secession of the plebs, which is undoubtedly historical, can have been directed only against the patricians as a body, and its object must have been to protect plebeian rights endangered by the patricians. Now, as we are informed that after the secession the office of tribunes was restored along with all the rights granted at the first secession, it seems a natural conclusion that the patricians had intended altogether to suppress the tribuneship, which had been only suspended during the decemvirate. Perhaps the patricians argued that now, after the decemviral legislation, the plebeian tribunes were no longer wanted, as the law itself would henceforth protect the plebeians. But the plebeians insisted on the restoration of the sacred laws, and they obtained it.

Criticism of the story.

A strong argument for the view we have taken of the second secession lies in the character of the laws, contained in the last two tables. These laws are universally described as unjust to the plebeians, and they contained the prohibition of marriages between the two orders of citizens, a prohibition which was really a badge of servitude and a remnant of the old inequality of patricians and plebeians. It ought not to have been received into the new code and could not have been sanctioned, as is alleged, by men who, like Appius Claudius and the second decemvirs, favoured the plebeians. On the other hand, the patricians, who made peace with the plebeians, did not repeal this obnoxious law. If they had been the real friends of the people, they could not have shown this in a more signal manner than by condemning a law so unpopular. As they did not do so, we may infer that they intentionally upheld that law; and we are only going one step further if we surmise that they introduced it into the code in opposition to the policy of Appius Claudius. This conclusion is confirmed by a statement of Diodorus, who says that the last two tables of laws were added by the consuls Valerius and Horatius, who succeeded the decemvirs.

The laws of the last two tables.

The result of these considerations is that in all probability the second decemvirs were opposed to the policy of the extreme patrician party, that they intended to carry out that equalisation of the laws which was the object of the Terentilian Rogation; that in this endeavour they were thwarted by the senate, which compelled them to resign before the last two tables were sanctioned; that the senate then embodied in the last two tables those old prohibitions of intermarriage between patricians and plebeians which were so offensive to the latter, and tried

Probable causes of the overthrow of the decemvirs.

CH. XVIII.   *Decemviral Legislation.*   169

to restore the old consular government without the **tribuneship of the people**; that thereupon the plebeians had recourse to a secession, and did not return until the sacred laws and the tribuneship had been restored to them. All the stories of violence and cruelty ascribed to the decemvirs must be regarded as fictitious, and as invented from the same motive of blackening the character of popular leaders, to which are to be ascribed similar charges brought against **Spurius Cassius**, Marcus Manlius, and even Caius Gracchus.

CHAPTER XIX.

EXTENSION OF PLEBEIAN RIGHTS FROM 449 TO 390 B.C.

THE laws of the Twelve Tables were not intended to be a reform of the constitution. They referred to the private rights of the citizens alone, especially to the civil law. The constitution of the republic was not touched by them, and was left entirely what it had been before. But the violent commotions which accompanied the downfall of the decemviral legislators, and which at one time threatened a dissolution of the commonwealth, involved a formal restoration of the old order of things, which was accompanied by a few slight modifications and new legal guarantees.

Bearing of the decemviral legislation on public and private laws.

In the first place the annual consulship was re-established. But the functions of treasurer or paymaster (quaestor), which had hitherto been discharged by a nominee of the consul, were now entrusted to an annual officer, elected by popular suffrage. By this means a check was imposed on the disposal of the public money by the consul. The

Quaestors elected by the people.

quaestor, though still acting under the authority of the consul, and looked upon as his subordinate, had to superintend the military expenditure and to account for the disposal of booty taken in war. He had to lay his accounts before the senate, the body which had the chief control of the public finances.

The consulship was restored subject to the old restrictions. The right of appeal from the consul's decisions to the popular assembly was guaranteed by a special enactment, which provided that no magistrate whatever should be elected unrestrained by this safeguard of popular liberty. As by the decemviral legislation the private rights of the plebeians and patricians had been equalised, the right of appeal was now probably extended to the plebeians.

Right of appeal confirmed and extended.

The tribuneship and aedileship were also restored, with their privilege of inviolability and the right of intercession. Special precautions were taken to secure the uninterrupted succession of tribunes, so that the people might never be in want of their legal protectors.

Restoration of the tribuneship and aedileship.

Finally, a law passed by the consuls Valerius and Horatius acknowledged the plebeian assembly of tribes as a sovereign assembly of the Roman people. It laid down the rule 'that the whole Roman people should be legally bound by the decisions of the tribes.' Whether this important law was an enactment entirely new in substance, or only the formal acknowledgment of an existing plebeian right, and as such a part of the general restoration of the old constitution, we are not informed. The latter, however, seems the most probable hypothesis, for in reality the plebeians must have been acknowledged as possessing the right of 'legally binding the whole Roman people' by their decisions from the moment when the

Sovereignty of the assembly of tribes acknowledged.

tribunes elected by them were invested with a public authority, to which the consuls themselves had to bow. The legislative sovereignty of the plebeian tribes was now extended more and more. It superseded gradually the legislation of the older comitia centuriata, which preserved only their rights of electing the consuls and (afterwards) the praetors and censors, the right of deciding on peace and war, and the supreme criminal legislation in cases of appeal.

The assembly of tribes, on the other hand, became now the only engine for legislative enactments, and was even empowered to elect those inferior magistrates who were subsequently appointed, such as quaestors and aediles. Again, questions of foreign as well as domestic policy were henceforth submitted to the decision of the plebeian assembly of tribes; so that the centre of gravity which had originally lain in the patrician assembly of curies, and then in the mixed assembly of centuries, was finally shifted entirely to the plebeian comitia of tribes. *Extension of the legislative and elective functions of the assembly of tribes.*

But this change was not effected at once. It was the slow result of a gradual abolition of all political privileges attaching to the patrician body. When the old consular constitution was restored, after the decemvirate, these privileges still existed entire, though the time was come when they were destined to fall one after another. *Gradual abolition of patrician privileges.*

First of all, the law against intermarriage between the two classes of citizens was abolished on the motion of a tribune of the people, called C. Canuleius (445 B.C.). This law, which seems to have caused so much heartburning and to have been a bone of contention in the second year of the decemvirate, was really no advantage to the patricians, but on the contrary a cause of *Canuleian law on the intermarriage of patricians and plebeians.*

weakness, as it prevented the aristocracy from gaining strength by the infusion of new blood. It can have been nothing but a narrow-minded religious scruple which opposed mixed marriages, under the impression that only a certain number of families enjoyed that special favour of the gods which secured divine protection to the state administered by them; that they alone could approach the gods by augury, and 'possess the *auspicia*'—be, as it were, the mediators between gods and men, a priesthood by birth, propagated only by purity of blood and intermarriage among themselves alone. How much these religious scruples were affected and supported by self-interest, we have no external evidence to decide. But it is not at all improbable that they were strengthened by the fact that political power and material advantages were bound up with the exclusive religious sanctity claimed by the patrician houses.

This exclusive possession of political power by the patricians was the tower of strength against which the plebeians henceforth directed their attacks. Hitherto, as we have seen, they had only claimed equality of private rights and protection from wrong. They had obtained the latter in their tribunes, and the former in the decemviral legislation, to which the Canuleian law of marriage must be looked upon as an appendix. In the very same

<small>Agitation for a share in the executive.</small> year (445 B.C.) the tribunes brought in a bill to sanction the election of plebeian consuls. The patricians resisted with all their might, but they were only able to alter the form and not the substance of the proposal. They objected to plebeian <small>The office of military tribunes with consular power.</small> consuls, but consented to the election of chief magistrates 'with consular power,' to be called 'military tribunes,' three in number, and eligible promiscuously from the two orders of citizens. What they proposed to gain, or did gain, by

Extension of Plebeian Rights.

this change in title is not quite clear. They cannot have been so childish as to fight a political battle for a mere name. It is probable that the military tribunes were considered as, in rank, inferior to the consuls, and that they lacked some of the attributes and rights which the consuls possessed. At the same time, the increase in the number of chief magistrates implies that one of the three was intended to discharge the duties of chief judge, for which afterwards a praetor was elected, and that the patricians reserved to themselves the right of filling this office with one of their own number. The other two military tribunes, whose principal duty was the command of the army, were to be elected indiscriminately from patricians and plebeians, and the important reservation was made that the government of the republic should be entrusted to consuls whenever the senate should deem it advisable. The consuls of course could be taken from the patrician body alone, and it was therefore left to the decision of the senate whether the new law was to be applied or not.

Even with these restrictions and modifications the apparent gain of the plebeians was very important. But unfortunately for them their opponents did not act with good faith and succeeded in making their concessions almost nugatory.

As the law now stood, the policy of the patricians was directed to two points: first, to obtain a decree of the senate for the election of consuls, and if this could not be carried, to make such good use of their influence in the comitia of centuries as to secure the election of patricians for the office of military tribunes, to the exclusion of plebeians. *Policy of the patricians to make the laws nugatory.*

For a considerable time the patricians were entirely successful. During the period between 444 B.C. and 409 B.C.

—that is, for thirty-five years—they managed to prevent the election of military tribunes and to substitute consuls not less than twenty times; and up to the year 400 B.C.—*i.e.* for twenty-three years—in which they were compelled to yield to the demands of the plebeians and to allow the election of military tribunes instead of consuls, they frustrated the success of plebeian candidates. For nearly half a century therefore—*i.e.* from 445 to 400—the victory which the plebeians had gained turned out to be really barren of results. Whether consuls or military tribunes directed the government, they were always taken from the patrician order, although the law sanctioned the election of plebeians at least for one of these offices.

The explanation of this curious circumstance seems at first sight very difficult. How could the plebeians rest satisfied with an apparent victory, with a mere change in the law, without following it up practically by enforcing the law? If they were strong enough to compel their opponents to surrender a privilege after a stubborn contest, could they lack the strength to appropriate the spoils? The truth seems to be, that a reaction took place after the great constitutional struggle in the time of the decemvirate, and that the equalisation and codification of the law which were effected at that period removed many of the grievances of the plebeian body. Moreover, the party in possession of the government, with all the influence of nobility, wealth, political experience and organization, was not easily beaten at elections if it chose to exert the whole of its power. This the Roman patricians were determined to do. In the senate they were all-powerful; in fact, the senate was as yet unpolluted by plebeian members. In the comitia centuriata they must have possessed a working majority either by their own votes or by the votes of their dependents and adherents. If these could

Explanation of this result.

not be trusted, the patricians had it in their power to influence the elections through a presiding magistrate of their own order, who might refuse to accept votes for an opposition candidate, or might adjourn the election, if he feared it would go against his party. He might even refuse to declare a plebeian duly elected, on the pretext of some irregularity. The auspices might be made use of as a political weapon; the gods might declare, through the mouth of a patrician augur, that they were not satisfied with the result of an election; the senate might withhold the 'patrum auctoritas;' or, finally, the patrician comitia curiata might object to confer upon a plebeian magistrate the 'imperium,' without which he could not lawfully take the command of the army. Such a copious store of political weapons explains sufficiently the continued ascendency of the patrician body, in spite of the temporary success gained by the plebeians at a time of great political excitement.

Nevertheless, there are indications of very severe struggles during this period. It seems that the patricians did not scruple to resort to violent measures when opposed by plebeian candidates of more than average ability or determination. On such occasions they did not shrink even from murder, as we learn from the fate of Spurius Maelius.

Ten years after the decemvirate (439 B.C.) dearth and famine desolated the land. The people suffered grievously, though a special commissioner of markets (*praefectus annonae*) was appointed to buy up corn for the supply of the people. In this emergency Spurius Maelius, a rich plebeian, came forward as a benefactor of the poor, distributed corn gratis, or at very low prices, and made himself so popular that the people appeared inclined to raise him to the consulship if he desired that honour. The patricians

<small>Spurius Maelius.</small>

suspected him of even greater ambition; at least they pretended to fear that he was planning the overthrow of the republic and the establishment of a monarchy. Upon information given by the commissioner of markets, that secret meetings were held at the house of Maelius, and that arms were being collected, a dictator was appointed, as in times of imminent danger, to save the republic. Cincinnatus, the conqueror of the Aequians, was the man selected. He set up his tribunal in the Forum, and sent Servilius Ahala, his master of the horse, to summon Maelius before him. Maelius, foreseeing the danger which threatened him, implored the protection of the people, whereupon Ahala drew a dagger and stabbed him to death, and Cincinnatus, as dictator, justified the deed. The people were terrified and cowed for the moment, but they soon recovered confidence, and Servilius Ahala was driven into exile and his property confiscated.

The violent proceeding against such a popular man as Spurius Maelius was perhaps not isolated. It shows that party spirit ran high in Rome at this time, and that the patricians were still strong enough to thwart the endeavours of the plebeians and to keep them out of offices which they had a legal right to hold.

Meanwhile, an important modification was made in the organization of the government by the creation of the censorship in 443 B.C.

The censorship.

From the first establishment of the comitia centuriata it had been necessary to classify the citizens of Rome according to their property. The assessments necessary for this purpose were made by the chief magistrates from time to time, as necessity or expediency seemed to require. It is probable that these duties were imperfectly discharged by the consuls, who had so much other work on hand, and that the census, which ought to have taken place at regular periods was often postponed under the pressure of war or internal disputes. It was but natural that with an increasing tendency to organize the different branches of the administration as separate magistracies, the duties of the censorship should at last be assigned to an officer elected for that special purpose, just as the quæstorship and afterwards the practorship were established as distinct from the consulship. The establishment of the censorship in 443 B.C. is only one feature of that general tendency to multiply magistracies by which the simplicity of the original republic was expanded into the elaborate organization of a more advanced period. Why the year 443 was chosen for the creation of the censorship is not recorded; but probably we shall not err if we look upon the reform as a result of the changes consequent upon the decemviral legislation, and, in particular, of the law which substituted military tribunes, eligible from patricians and plebeians alike, for the original patrician consuls. The patricians naturally wished to keep the management of public affairs as much as possible in their own hands, and they reserved to their own order the eligibility to the new office of censor. They succeeded in keeping exclusive possession of it for nearly 100 years. In 351 B.C. the first plebeian censor was elected, and not until 339 B.C. was a formal law passed to secure the regular election of one plebeian to the office.

In creating the new office of censors the Romans followed the practice established for the consuls and quaestors, of electing not one, but two magistrates to act as colleagues. The motive must have been as in the older cases—the wish to allow one censor, by his intercession, to control the action of the other, a motive amply justified by experience. As a census could not be taken every year, the censorship differed from the other republican offices

Duration of the office of censors.

in point of duration. It was made to extend over five years; the intention being that once in that period, which, from the religious ceremony of lustration (*i.e.* purification) of the people, the Romans called a *lustrum*, a new valuation of property should take place, and that every Roman citizen should have the place assigned according to which he had to vote and to contribute to the burdens of the state.

The lists of citizens drawn up by the censors thus became the authentic registers recognized by the state. No Extent of the power of the censors in drawing up the list of citizens. man could claim the rights of a Roman citizen whose name was not on their lists, and the constitutional privileges possessed by Roman magistrates were such that on the occasion of the census the censors, acting with a discretion almost despotic, were allowed to transfer citizens to other classes or tribes, or even to exclude them altogether, and to admit freedmen to the rank of citizens,—in fact, to remodel the community, to alter even the principles on which the census was based, and thus to adapt the old institutions to the varying conditions of the times. It was natural that the original sums fixed as the census of different classes should not remain a correct standard for a long period, and that the mode of assessment had to be modified as the habits of life and the views held on the value of personal or real property were changed. Thus, the censors were, in point of fact, the agents for periodical reforms, and prevented the necessity of a sweeping reform bill—such as that which was passed in England in 1832 to reconcile the principle of representation which suited the fifteenth century to the altered economical and social conditions of the nineteenth.

But the censors were not confined to drawing up the lists of private citizens alone. A duty, if not more im portant, certainly more calculated to give them weight with the nobility, was the periodical renewal of the senate. The members of that body, as we have seen, were not elected by the people, like those of the House of Commons, nor were they hereditary, like those of the House of Lords; they were nominated by the executive, *i.e.* by the kings in that early period which we call regal, and by the consuls after the establishment of the republic. Upon the establishment of the censorship this nomination was made to devolve on the censors. They had to draw up a list of the senators, and it was left to their discretion to add new members in the place of those deceased, and also to strike out the names of men whom they considered unworthy of the great honour and responsibility of a seat in that august assembly. As a rule the senators were nominated for life; but the law, by sanctioning a periodical revision of the senatorial list, enabled the censors to exclude men notoriously unworthy. If this important duty had been exercised in a reckless party spirit, so that the censors had ejected the members of what we should call the Opposition, the Roman senate would inevitably have lost that character of a fixed and settled institution which enabled it in the good old times to control all parties and to direct the public policy with a view only to the national interest. Every election of censors would have become a test of the strength of parties, and the victorious party would each time have excluded its opponents from a share in the government. A periodical oscillation would have been the result in the policy of Rome, such as we are accustomed to see in modern constitutional governments. But the evils of such an oscillation would have been much greater in Rome than they are in a state where the crown represents the permanent national interests, which are above the interests of conflicting parties.

<small>Nomination of senators.</small>

180 *Early Rome.* CH. XIX.

Besides the general list of Roman citizens and the list of senators, the censors had to draw up a list of the knights. The centuries of knights formed a part of that organization known as the constitution of centuries, generally attributed to Servius Tullius. Originally, the centuries of knights or horsemen, eighteen in number, were intended to contain the young men fit for cavalry service in the army, and the cavalry of the legions continued to be made up chiefly of the men thus selected by the censors. But as the assembly of centuries gradually lost its military character and became a purely political body, the centuries of knights assumed more and more the character of a select body of citizens, distinct from the great mass by wealth and connexion. Knighthood began to be looked upon as a preliminary stage to the senatorial rank and as constituting an intermediate class. It comprised the young men of the noble houses, though, as far as we know, no property qualification was exacted for membership before the time of the Gracchi. It was more and more considered an honour to belong to the centuries of knights; and as they counted eighteen votes in the centuriate assembly, and also enjoyed the right of voting before the others, they possessed great influence. Hence, older men who had served their time in the army, and even senators, found it desirable to retain their votes in the centuries of knights, and the censorial discretion in drawing up these lists was one of great importance.

Revision of the centuries of knights.

From the exercise of these rights the censors acquired in course of time a power much coveted and highly valued—the power of sitting in judgment on the civic virtue of all Roman citizens, of punishing misconduct by exclusion from public rights and honours. They acquired what was called the *censura morum,* the censorship of morals, which supplied

The censorship of morals.

a defect in the code of laws, and in that code of public decency and social propriety which in our own time is successfully enforced by public opinion, aided by the press. As the full exercise of this moral judicature of the censors belongs to a later period, we need not here dwell upon it any longer.

In the censorial functions of classifying the citizens according to their property was contained the germ of their financial duties. They obtained in course of time the control of the public income and expenditure, especially with regard to the revenue from domain lands and to the outlay on public works. The full development of these financial duties, however, belongs to a later period. Financial duties of the censors.

When the censorship had been tried for two lustral periods it was found necessary, in 434 B.C., to modify the tenure of office and to limit its duration to one year and a half; but probably the motive for this change was not the wish to limit the legitimate power and authority of the office. Limitation of the censorship to eighteen months. It is quite evident that such a process as a census ought always to be accomplished in the shortest possible period. If the censors took full five years before they completed their lists of citizens, knights, and senators, and assessed the property of each, they not only held the whole community in suspense for all this long period and thereby produced a feeling of insecurity, but they ran the risk of publishing statistical data not in accordance with actual facts.

In the year 421 B.C. the principle of multiplying the number of chief magistrates, in the interest of the public service and in that of the plebeians, received a further illustration by the doubling of the number of quaestors. It was arranged that both patricians and plebeians should be eligible. No Doubling of the number of quaestors.

doubt the patricians expected to get their own candidates elected as regularly for this office as for the military tribuneship. But in this expectation they were deceived. The election took place, not like that of military tribunes and consuls in the assembly of centuries, but in that of tribes, and in these the patricians had not the same influence as in the other assembly. Consequently we find that as early as 410 B.C. three quaestors out of four were plebeians.

This was the first triumph of the plebeians. Soon after (in 400, 399, and 396 B.C.) they carried the election of several plebeian military tribunes, and thus for the first time realized the privilege which they had won about half a century before. They never again lost the ground thus gained, and in less than ten years more (388 B.C.) they reached at last the long-desired end of political equality, by the Licinian laws, which gave them a share in the consulship. However, before this great constitutional change took place, the commonwealth of Rome passed through a series of dangers from foreign enemies, which, more than any internal disturbances, threatened it with dissolution.

<small>Plebeians elected to the office of military tribunes.</small>

CHAPTER XX.

THE FOREIGN RELATIONS OF ROME DOWN TO THE CONQUEST OF VEII.

WHILE, in the constitutional struggles of the people of Rome, political rights were more and more equally distributed among all her citizens, while the republic was being consolidated, and the administration improved and developed through a succession of reforms, the relations of Rome with her neighbours

<small>The position of Rome in Latium.</small>

remained substantially unaltered, and her influence in Italy was not perceptibly increased. She continued to be one of the Latin cities—the largest of them, it is true, and the most powerful—but still her voice was probably never heard beyond the confines of Latium and the territories of her immediate neighbours. All her energies were required to maintain the ground she already occupied, and to ward off the hereditary enemies who year after year assailed her and her allies, and sometimes succeeded in penetrating to her very walls.

The league with the Latins and Hernicans subsisted in form and substance, though the allies of Rome were no longer the unbroken people they had been when the league was concluded. Some of the Latin cities, such as Corioli, lay in ruins; others had fallen into the hands of the Volscians. Tusculum was kept in a state of almost perpetual alarm by the Aequians, who had established a footing on Mount Algidus, one of the spurs of the Alban Mount, overlooking the plain of Latium. Praeneste, probably the strongest Latin town after Rome, had become virtually an independent town and detached from the league. It is clear that this league was in a state of gradual dissolution, and that Rome became more and more isolated and exposed. *Condition of Latium.*

Fortunately this progress of destruction was arrested. In the second half of the fifth century (from 450 to 400 B.C.) the attacks of the Aequians and Volscians became by degrees feebler. Whether it was that their strength was spent, or that they themselves were now exposed in their rear to the attack of a fiercer mountain tribe (the Samnites), Rome and her allies obtained breathing time; and as the internal dissensions between patricians and plebeians had been to some extent allayed by the decemviral legislation and the reforms which followed, the attention of the republic *Decay of the Volscians and Aequians* could be successfully turned abroad, and Rome was able to profit by the favourable change.

It was natural that the calamities of war should press more heavily on the Latin cities, which surrounded Rome like so many outlying bulwarks, than on Rome itself. Had the tide of war not been stemmed, Rome would in the end have been swept away herself, but now she actually profited by the losses of her allies; for her preponderance increased so greatly that she became in fact the head and mistress of those who had previously been in reality and still were in name her allies on equal terms. It does not seem that Rome made a very generous use of this altered position. At least, if we can judge of her general policy from an isolated instance, we shall not be inclined to rate the public morality of Rome very high. The city of Corioli was one of those ancient members of the league which had been utterly destroyed in the Volscian wars. The land which had formed the territory of Corioli lay between the two cities of Ardea and Aricia, and these cities wrangled and actually fought for the possession of the deserted land. At last (in 446 B.C.) they applied to Rome to settle the dispute, and the result was that Rome claimed and occupied the disputed land for herself. This was not a very honourable transaction, and the Roman historians themselves, who report it, seem heartily ashamed of it. Livy does not hesitate to call it a monument of public shame. It shows what Rome could now venture to do; and it is interesting to note that this acquisition of the territory of Corioli was the first extension of the Roman dominions, after the establishment of the republic, of which we know. It was the iniquitous beginning of a national policy which throughout retained the same character of rapacity and bad faith with which it was begun.

Increased preponderance of Rome.

Acquisition of the territory of Corioli.

The next acquisitions were made on the eastern side of Rome. In 418 B.C. the town of Labici, which had been originally Latin and a member of the league, but which had been for some time in the hands of the Aequians, was at length retaken. The same success attended the Roman arms four years later (414 B.C.), when Bolae, a town still further east, was taken from the Aequians. About the same time the Volscians seem to have lost several of the towns which they had previously conquered in Latium, and it is even related that a Roman army marched southward right through the land of the Volscians, and took the maritime town of Anxur, which was afterwards called Terracina.

Conquest of Labici, Bolae, and other towns in Latium.

Even more significant than these signs of returning strength in the wars with their eastern and southern foes, the Aequians and Volscians, was the spirit shown by the Romans in a conflict which now broke out with the Etruscans, and which led, after a severe and protracted struggle, to the first great conquest of a large fortified town that could rival Rome itself in extent, population, and power—the great Etruscan city of Veii.

Even before the important conquest of Labici had been made (418 B.C.) the Romans had succeeded in clearing away, on the left bank of the Tiber, the last remnant of the old ascendency of the Etruscans, by the conquest and destruction (in 426) of the small town of Fidenae (p. 156). In this war, Aulus Cornelius Cossus, the Roman master of the horse, slew, it is said, with his own hand Lars Tolumnius, the Veientine king, who had come to the aid of Fidenae, and, as was customary in Rome, he dedicated the spoils in the temple of Jupiter Feretrius on the Capitol. The spoils of Lars Tolumnius were the first *spolia opima*, i.e. spoils of a hostile commander slain by a Roman commander, since Romulus

Conquest of Fidenae.

The spolia opima of Cornelius Cossus.

had slain Acron, the king of Antemnae. They were still in existence in the time of Augustus, whose attention was drawn to them when he caused the temple of Jupiter Feretrius to be repaired. We are told by Livy that it was Augustus himself who informed him that the inscription upon the coat-of-arms of Tolumnius designated Cornelius Cossus as consul, and not as master of the horse. It appears, therefore, that if the said inscription was genuine and correctly read, the war with Fidenae must have taken place not in 426 B.C., when A. Cornelius Cossus was master of the horse, but in 428, when he was consul.

Whatever we may think of the chronological doubts thus created, it is at any rate certain, that about this time Fidenae was taken by the Romans. It seems to have been utterly destroyed, and it was never rebuilt, for in the age of Horace and Juvenal Fidenae is alluded to as the picture of desolation and loneliness.

The conquest of Fidenae was in itself important enough, as it delivered Rome from a very troublesome neighbour in its immediate vicinity. But it proved only the first step to a far more valuable acquisition on the side of Etruria.

At a distance of about ten miles to the north of Rome was situated the large and powerful city of Veii, strongly fortified by nature and art. Veii was decidedly the leading town in southern Etruria, and probably occupied a position similar to that which Rome held in Latium. She was far superior to Rome in wealth and arts, and perhaps not inferior in public spirit and military organization. Her architects, sculptors, and artizans found employment in Rome, and first familiarized the ruder inhabitants of Latium with the more refined enjoyments and tastes of civilized life. In spite of this peaceful intercourse the geographical proximity of the two towns made a hostile collision in the long run inevit-

The city of Veii.

able, and a serious war could end only in the destruction of one of the two, since the difference of their nationality and language made a peaceful amalgamation difficult or impossible.

In the war which led to the destruction of Fidenae the Veientines, as we have seen, had taken a part. Peace was concluded between the two states, and the Veientines seem to have kept quiet while Rome secured her ascendency in Latium by the conquest of Labici and Bolae and by successful wars with the Volscians. This peace lasted till 406 B.C. Of the causes which led to a renewal of hostilities we know nothing. It is not unlikely that Rome engaged in the war as the ally and protector of some of the towns subject to Veii, especially Sutrium and Nepete; for we find that these towns were, after the destruction of Veii, the allies of Rome, and it was quite consistent with the spirit of Roman policy to interfere in the internal disputes of her neighbours and to act the popular part of the protector of innocence against oppression, *i.e.* of the weaker against the stronger, provided a material advantage could be obtained.

<small>Hostilities between Veii and Rome.</small>

About the same time the northern towns of Etruria were alarmed by the approach of the Gauls, who had recently crossed the Alps, invaded the north of Italy, and, after having overrun the plain of the Po, gradually fought their way southwards to the more genial and fertile regions of central and southern Italy.

Owing to this fatal circumstance Veii was left destitute of the support of her allies in the north, and being thus isolated offered a tempting prize to the cupidity of the Romans.

Whatever may have been the origin and cause of the war, the Romans, once engaged in it, carried it on with a perseverance and singleness of purpose which they had never shown before on such a scale, but which was eminently characteristic of their nation.

Feeling that their military organization was deficient, they set about reforming it, and availed themselves of the services of a man, who rose at the right moment to direct the energies of his countrymen. This man was Marcus Furius Camillus, a hero destined to accomplish the victory over the mightiest enemy which Rome had as yet encountered, to be fondly called by his countrymen the second founder of Rome, and to close a long and glorious life by aiding in the great work of establishing concord between the hostile ranks of citizens.

New military organization of Camillus.

The Roman legions, as we know, did not consist of mercenaries, serving for pay, nor of volunteers, induced to take arms by their own free patriotic impulse. They consisted of citizens, who in defending their country were performing the primary and most important civic duty. For the discharge of this duty they received no remuneration. The burthens connected with it they had themselves to pay from their own means. The richer citizens were called upon to provide themselves with the more costly armour required by the men in the front ranks, and of course they had to bear the brunt of battle. As compensation for these services, they had a greater number of votes in the popular assembly. It was evident that with such a military organization the lowest ranks of the citizens could not have been called upon to take any part in the national defence, or else that their services must have been very subordinate. In progress of time the military duties were found to press too heavily upon the rich, and a more equal distribution was necessary. The old division of classes and the old difference of arms were modified. The soldiers of the legions were divided into two classes

The Roman armies.

only—the heavy-armed and the light-armed. The arms were furnished by the state, and consequently the comitia of centuries, which continued to be a political body, ceased to be a military organization. Up to the Veientine war, however, the soldier received no regular pay, and in consequence it was unfair and impossible to keep the men for a long time away from their domestic pursuits, from their fields and workshops. The campaigns could not be extended beyond a few weeks or months in summer. No military operation, therefore, could be undertaken which required a long period of service. On the approach of winter, if not before, the men had to be dismissed to their homes, and new armies had to be formed on the return of spring. Now such a procedure might suit the desultory warfare which consisted in making occasional inroads for the sake of plunder; but a serious war with a powerful state, especially the siege of a large town, required armies of a more permanent character—armies that were not disbanded in the autumn, or disbanded only to be immediately replaced by newly-levied forces. To accomplish this it was necessary to provide the soldiers with the means of bearing the burden of military service, and consequently to pay them from the public treasury. This was done in the last war with Veii by the advice of Camillus. It was a measure calculated to work a great change in the military system of the Romans, and to exercise great influence also on political affairs and on the state of parties. It served to equalise the rich and the poor, and it acted therefore as a powerful stimulus in bringing to a final settlement the long-continued struggle of the patricians and the plebeians.

Introduction of military pay.

With their newly-organized armies the Romans laid siege to the city of Veii and kept it blockaded summer and winter. But the fortune of war was variable. More than once the Veientines broke through the besieging army and carried the war into the vicinity of Rome. We hear of defeats sustained by the Roman legions. The war was protracted to the tenth year. At length Furius Camillus was appointed dictator, and he soon led the legions to victory.

Siege of Veii.

That Veii was taken by the Romans under Camillus is a fact beyond dispute. But the mode of its conquest is hidden in a cloud of fables. We are told that in the course of the war the Alban lake rose miraculously to such a height that it threatened to flood the whole plain of Latium. The Romans, looking upon this phenomenon as a sign sent from the gods, were informed by an Etruscan soothsayer and also by the Delphian oracle, that if they constructed a channel to draw off the water of the lake they would obtain possession of the hostile town. They immediately set to work, constructed a channel in the side of the hill, and thus permanently lowered the level of the lake, making the water at the same time available for irrigating the plain below. While this work was in progress they continued the siege of Veii. Here also they availed themselves of tunnelling. Camillus caused an underground passage to be constructed from his camp right into the citadel of Veii. When this was finished he caused the attention of the besieged to be divested by sham attacks on the walls, whilst with a chosen band he penetrated through the tunnel into the town and came out in the very temple of Juno, the protecting deity of Veii, at the moment when the king was in the act of offering up sacrifice, and when the priest had just exclaimed that this sacrifice was a pledge of victory. At that auspicious moment Camillus, we are told, broke into the temple, snatched the offering from the hands of the king, and flung it into the fire on

Miraculous capture of Veii.

the altar. The Romans, issuing from the tunnel, fell upon the rear of the Veientines, opened the gates, let in their comrades, and obtained possession of the town. Veii was taken and sacked. The people who did not fall in battle were led away as captives and sold as slaves. The victorious army returned laden with spoils, and Camillus, mounted on a car drawn by white horses, and dressed in the garments of Jupiter, celebrated a triumph such as had never been witnessed before.

But a great reverse was in store both for the victorious leader and for his people. In vain had Camillus in the moment of victory attempted to avert the jealousy of the gods by a fervent prayer that, if they thought him guilty of overweening pride, they should inflict a merciful punishment. Whilst he uttered this prayer he had his head veiled, as was customary, and turning round on his feet, he stumbled and fell to the ground. This slight mishap he fondly hoped had conciliated the gods. But he soon found out his error. Instead of gratitude he reaped hatred and persecution. He was charged with having unjustly appropriated a part of the spoils, with having exhibited impious pride and presumption because of the pomp displayed in his triumph, and with depriving the people of the fruits of their victory, by inducing the senate to pass a decree that the tenth part of all the spoils should be dedicated as an offering to the Delphian Apollo. So great was the animosity of the people against him that he was compelled to leave Rome and to go into exile.

Such is the wonderful account of the capture of Veii and of the exploits and the fate of Camillus. That it is fictitious in all its details needs no proof. It was evidently made up at a time when the actual facts were forgotten, and it was made up by men who had more talent for dramatic composition than for

<small>Criticism of the story.</small>

historical research—men who were not even familiar with the laws and habits of the Roman people. The charge, for instance, that Camillus committed sacrilege by assuming the garb of Jupiter, when he entered Rome in triumph, is utterly futile. We know that this was the habit of all the Roman *triumphatores*. By personating, as it were, Jupiter, they were far from any sinful arrogance or impiety. On the contrary, they intended thereby to imply that it was Jupiter himself who triumphed over the enemies of Rome. The idea of Veii being taken by a tunnel, driven through the rocky hill into the midst of the town, is simply ridiculous, and was perhaps suggested by the notion that the channel for the water of the Alban lake was the cause of the fall of Veii. Whether this channel was actually constructed or only repaired at that time, we have no means of knowing. It certainly did exist, and exists even now; but except in the superstition of an ignorant age it could have no connexion with the capture of a distant town. The message to the oracle of Delphi is no doubt only a late version of the older story, which attributes the prophecy to an Etruscan soothsayer; nor does the statement deserve credit that the tenth part of the Veientine spoils were sent as a present to the Delphian shrine, although it is adorned with detail intended to make it plausible. At the period in question the Romans had perhaps not even heard of the Delphian Apollo, and certainly never dreamt of consulting him, nor of sending him golden offerings.

Thus nothing can be really ascertained but the bare fact that in the year 396 B.C. the city of Veii was, after a protracted siege, taken by the Romans. We do not even know certainly whether Rome was aided in this magnificent conquest by any other Etruscan towns. But as we hear that Sutrium and Nepete, to the north of Veii, were afterwards the allies of Rome, we may at any rate conjecture that they had a part in the subversion of Veii. Other cities of Etruria may have taken a part in the war. Tarquinii and Caere appear to have been neutral, but Capena and Falerii are mentioned as allies of the Veientines. Falerii, after the fall of Veii, was implicated in hostilities with Rome. A story better known than it deserves to be is related of this war. Camillus, it is said, laid siege to the town. During this siege a schoolmaster of Falerii treacherously delivered into his hands a number of noble children as hostages, but was ignominiously sent back into the town to be punished for his intended treason. The Faliscans, overcome not by the arms but by the generosity of their foe, surrendered. This story is condemned as a silly fiction, not only by its intrinsic improbability, but by the undoubted fact that Falerii continued for a long time afterwards to be an independent town.

The territory acquired by the conquest of Veii was about equal to the old possessions of Rome in extent and fertility. It offered a magnificent field to Roman colonists for, according to the custom of ancient warfare, it was entirely at the disposal of the conquerors, who could appropriate as much of it as they thought expedient. A part was actually distributed in equal lots of seven *jugera* to Roman settlers. The majority of the Veientine citizens who were not killed or sold, or left to till the soil, were transported as slaves to Rome, and may have proved a valuable accession of skilled workmen. Rome was evidently on the road to a rapid development when the Nemesis of the gods, whom Camillus had in vain attempted to propitiate, brought upon her a reverse which seemed hardly less terrible than the fate of Veii. Six years after the triumph of Camillus, Rome was a heap of ruins, and the Roman people, a homeless herd of exiles, were seeking shelter and refuge in the city of their late enemies.

A. H.   O

CHAPTER XXI.

THE INVASION OF THE GAULS.

THE large and fruitful plain in the north of Italy, extending on both sides of the Po from the Alps to the Adriatic and the Apennines, had been for some time in possession of the Etruscans, who had built and fortified twelve cities and lived in a sort of confederacy, similar to that which loosely bound together the towns of Etruria proper. Long before the rise of Rome the power of the Etruscans was at its height; their settlements extended from the Alps to Campania, and their ships swept the sea, which after them was called the Tyrrhenian. When Rome rose to independence and preponderance in Latium, the Etruscan power gradually declined. They lost Campania on the advance of the Sabellian races into that fertile plain. They were driven out of Latium by Rome and her Latin allies, and at the time when even the soil of Etruria proper was assailed and Veii, the most powerful Etruscan town in the south of that region, fell a prey to Rome, their settlements in the north were invaded by a more ruthless conqueror, and all the vestiges of Etruscan civilization in that beautiful plain of the Po were stamped out by the Gauls.

Decline of Etruscan power.

It is most probable that the inhabitants of Transalpine Gaul, the country which has now for centuries borne the name of France, had been accustomed in very early ages to cross the mountain ranges which separated them from Spain and Italy, for the purpose of plunder or permanent settlements in the more southern regions. In Spain they amalgamated with the native Iberian tribes and formed the mixed race known as Celtiberians. In Italy they expelled the former inhabitants from the country, which, after them, was called

Migration of the Gauls.

Cisalpine Gaul. These migrations and settlements were in all probability not effected by one wholesale exodus, but (like the Teutonic conquest of Britain) were the work of a long period of time, during which tribe after tribe followed the impulse given by the first adventurers.

At length, when the greater part of Cisalpine Gaul was filled by the new comers, the flood of migration was turned southwards. It filled the plain between the Apennines and the Adriatic, where the old Umbrian population gave way to the Gallic Senones; it mounted the passes of the Apennines, and at length came pouring down into the fertile valleys of Etruria proper. Five years after the capture of Veii by Camillus, a barbaric host appeared before the city of Clusium, a few days' march north of Rome. The danger had approached sufficiently near to rouse the attention of the Romans, even if they had been indifferent to the fate of their neighbours. *Their invasion of Etruria.*

Livy relates that the people of Clusium, in their extreme danger, sent ambassadors to implore the aid of Rome, and that the senate despatched three men of the noble house of the Fabii to expostulate with the Gauls, and to request them not to molest the allies of the Roman people. It is further related that the Gauls, not heeding the interference of a people of whom they had not even heard, attacked Clusium, and that the Fabii, forgetful of their sacred character of ambassadors, took part in the battle, and fought foremost in the ranks of the Etruscans; that upon this breach of the law of nations, the Gauls demanded the surrender of the ambassadors, and when this was refused by the Romans, forthwith abandoned the prosecution of hostilities against Clusium, and marched straight upon Rome. *Cause of war with Rome.*

This story, if not altogether fictitious, seems dressed

up to flatter the vanity of the Roman patriots. The language put in the mouth of the ambassadors savours of the arrogance which at a later period dictated the language of Roman diplomacy, when the power of Rome disdained the decencies of international politeness, and everywhere exhibited itself in its naked brutality. We prefer, therefore, the account of Diodorus, who tells us that the Romans did not send ambassadors, but spies. If this account is more correct, it follows that all about the participation of the Fabii in the fight, and their distinguished bravery, about the offence taken by the Gauls, and their message of expostulation to Rome,—in short, about all that is represented as a consequence of the breach of international law, falls to the ground. Nor, in truth, is it necessary to search for a particular reason why the Gauls should have marched upon Rome. They were on a plundering expedition. It was surely a sufficient inducement for them to attack the Romans, if they could hope to obtain their ends, and they were probably not too scrupulous in requiring a legitimate cause for war.

At any rate the Romans were not taken unawares. They had drawn out their whole strength, and were joined by their allies. Thus they marched out 40,000 strong to meet the invaders, who were advancing 70,000 strong along the left bank of the Tiber. Near the small river Allia the two armies met, about ten miles from Rome, on the fatal 18th of July, 390 B.C. The encounter was sharp, short, and decisive. The impetuous onset of the barbarians, their wild battle-cry, and their fierce, uncouth appearance dismayed the Romans, who, seized with a panic, fled almost without offering resistance. It was a slaughter more than a battle. Thousands rushed into the river to save themselves by swimming to the opposite bank, and many met their death in the waves. The consular tribune, A. Sul-

Battle of the Allia.

picius, with a remnant of the army, made good his retreat to Rome, while the greater part of the fugitives collected in Veii, the late rival of Rome, which, although overthrown, dismantled, and deserted, was now the only place of refuge for what remained of the Roman legions.

The Roman people never forgot the terrible day of the Allia. The 18th of July was marked as a black day in the Roman calendar, and was held unpropitious for any public undertaking. The terrible defeat and its more terrible consequences made such an impression on the public mind that the Gaul was ever afterwards dreaded as the most terrible of enemies.

On the third day after the fatal battle the victorious barbarians appeared before the city. The Romans instead of availing themselves of the respite thus given them, and of taking measures for the defence of the walls, thought of nothing but flight. *Rome abandoned.* They poured out of the city, carrying with them their most precious and easily transportable possessions, and sought refuge in the neighbouring towns. It is related that some of the sacred objects of the temples were secretly buried and that the vestal virgins, carrying with them the eternal flame from their sanctuary, hurried along with the crowd across the wooden bridge and up the Janiculus, until a plebeian citizen bade them mount a waggon on which he was conveying his wife and children from the general wreck.

When the Gauls found the walls destitute of defenders, they at first feared an ambush and hesitated for a while before breaking open the gates and penetrating into the deserted streets. They were appalled by the stillness which reigned as in a city of the dead. On advancing as far as the market-place they observed a number of venerable grey-bearded men sitting motionless like statues, dressed in robes of office. They were senators, who had determined not to survive the downfall of their country and who had devoted themselves to death. A Gaul, doubtful what to think of these figures, plucked one by the beard. A blow on his head from the offended senator convinced him that he had a living Roman before him, and a general massacre of all the devoted band was the consequence.

But besides these few defenceless old men other Romans had stayed behind. The Capitol had not been abandoned like the remainder of the city. It was garrisoned by a number of stout-hearted warriors, determined to conquer or fall in the defence of the sanctuary of Jupiter Capitolinus, the symbol and centre of the Roman power. They repelled an attack of the Gauls, and compelled them to trust to the slow effect of a regular siege, if they wished to reduce the place. Meanwhile the city was sacked by the barbarians and reduced to ashes. It is said that only a few houses on the Palatine escaped the general conflagration. In this sad calamity perished all or almost all the monuments of antiquity and the records of the past.

Defence of the Capitol.

The Gauls persisted in pressing the siege with a constancy hardly natural to such a restless and impatient race. The garrison on the Capitol seemed to be hopelessly lost, when one night a young man, called Pontius Cominius, sent from the Roman fugitives at Veii, made his way by swimming to a spot near the foot of the capitol, and, frustrating the watchfulness of the Gauls, scaled the rock at a place known to him as accessible to a nimble climber. He reported to the military tribune in command that the Roman force collected at Veii were about to come to the rescue of the besieged and that they only wanted the banished Camillus to be their leader. The decree recalling Camillus from banishment and appointing him dictator was made imme-

Camillus appointed dictator

diately, and Cominius hastened back the same way he had come.

His exploit, however, nearly proved fatal to the defenders of the capitol. The Gauls had noticed his footsteps on the rock, and following in the same track succeeded on a dark night in reaching the top unobserved by the Roman sentinels. Even the dogs were remiss in their watchfulness. Only the geese, kept in the temple of Juno, as birds sacred to the goddess, set up a loud cackling, and thus roused Marcus Manlius, one of the officers in charge. He immediately gave the alarm, and rushing to the spot where the foremost Gauls had already reached the top of the rock, he hurled them down upon their companions and thus saved the citadel. The Capitol saved by M. Manlius.

This danger was luckily averted, but the siege continued and the garrison on the capitol was sorely pressed. Provisions began to fail, as month after month elapsed and no rescue appeared. The blockade had now lasted six months. The Gauls, too, began to suffer from want of provisions. They were obliged to detach parts of their army for the purpose of collecting supplies. One of these bodies was set upon by the people of Ardea, under the command of Camillus, and routed with great slaughter. At length, Brennus, the leader of the Gauls, was fain to make an agreement with the Romans on the Capitol, and to promise to retire upon payment of a sum of money. One thousand pounds of gold was the ransom to be paid by the Roman people. The money was procured by borrowing the treasures from the temples and the ornaments of the Roman matrons. Ransom paid to the Gauls.

When the Roman commissioners were in the act of paying the gold to Brennus in the Forum, just at the foot of the Capitol, and when, upon their complaints of the false weight used by the Gauls, Brennus had just thrown his sword into the balance with the insulting words, 'Woe to the conquered!' Camillus suddenly appeared on the spot, and declaring that the agreement was null and void, because it had been concluded without the dictator's consent, drove the Gauls off the Forum and out of the city. On the next day he encountered them outside the gates, and routed them so signally that not a man escaped. Brennus himself fell under the sword of the conqueror, who shouted into his ears the terrible words he himself had first used in the insolence of victory, 'Woe to the conquered!' Thus Rome was saved not only from her foes but also from the disgrace of owing her deliverance to the payment of gold rather than to the sword; and Camillus restored to his country, became the second founder of the city.

Expulsion of the Gauls.

We have related the story of the capture and delivery of Rome in the form which it had assumed in Livy's time under the influence of patriotic tradition. We need hardly say that it is coloured by national and family pride, and that some of its features resemble more a theatrical catastrophe than sober reality. Fortunately in the narratives of Diodorus and Polybius some traces of an older and less falsified tradition have been preserved, by the help of which we can clear away some at least of the fictions of the later annalists.

Criticism of the story.

It is, at any rate, certain that the Gauls after their victory on the Allia entered Rome and destroyed the city with the exception of the Capitol. But we may doubt whether the destruction was so systematic and complete as it is generally represented—whether all the stone buildings and the walls of the city were pulled down after the combustible matter had been consumed by the flames. A regular destruction of solid masonry is a work

The destruction of Rome less complete than reported.

of time and great labour, such as would not be likely to be undertaken by invaders like the Gauls, who had no object in view but rapine and plunder. We know from Diodorus and Justin that the Gauls penetrated as far as Iapygia in the extreme south of Italy, and that some of them entered as mercenaries into the service of Dionysius of Syracuse, then at war with the Greek towns in Italy. Being bent on such distant enterprises, from which ample gain and booty were to be expected, how should they have been induced to waste their time and energy in pulling down what remained of the houses, temples, monuments, or walls, after they had ransacked them for treasures and committed them to the flames? Besides the walls and temples, Rome contained at that time very few solid structures. The majority of the private houses were mere straw-thatched or shingle-covered huts; yet even among the private buildings some may have been built at least in part of stone, and most of these may have survived the conflagration. Thus it is possible that even outside the Capitol a few monuments of antiquity were preserved, and that the ancient records were not so completely destroyed as the later annalists have reported.

We are the more fully justified in adopting this view, as we can hardly believe the statement that the Gauls encamped on the site of the ruins of Rome for seven months to press the siege of the Capitol. They could hardly have done so without exposing themselves to the most destructive effects of a climate, not merely unhealthy but deadly to a northern people. In fact, they would not have been barbarians, but madmen, if, with the prospect of a protracted siege before them, they had deliberately destroyed the shelter of which they would have felt such urgent need. We refer again to the testimony of Diodorus and

Long duration of the blockade improbable.

Justin, who speak of the extension of the Gallic invasion to southern Italy. With such a march southwards the blockade of the Capitol for seven months is incompatible, and cannot therefore be admitted as historical.

The oldest stories of the part played by Camillus seem to presuppose that the Gauls did not stay a very long time in the ruins of Rome. They represent Camillus as elected dictator and as in command of a Roman force outside the city. Surely, they could not look upon him as inactive for many months, or as engaged only in hovering on the outskirts of the territory occupied by the invaders. The story of Camillus is essentially dramatic in character. It brings the hero on the scene of action in a manner nothing short of marvellous, like a *deus ex machina*, and it would not have resulted to the honour of such a hero to wait seven months and to let his countrymen undergo the agonies of despair and famine before he came to their rescue.

The story of Camillus.

But after all the story of Camillus appears to be only a fiction invented for the glory of the Furian house to which Camillus belonged. Not to dwell on other points we will simply quote the testimony of Polybius, who says that 'the Gauls withdrew unmolested with their booty, having voluntarily and on their own terms restored the town to the Romans.' After this explicit statement what becomes of the heroic deeds of Camillus, of the unjust scales with the sword of Brennus, and of his expulsion from the Forum, which was so ignominious, and yet less ignominious than wonderful? It is clear that all the various and conflicting stories which relate the utter discomfiture of the Gauls and the recovery of the booty or ransom, are fictions calculated to soothe the wounded pride of the Romans and to glorify the family of Camillus.

Contradicted by Polybius.

Hardly less suspicious is the story of the Capitoline

geese and of M. Manlius, the saviour of the Capitol. They both belong to the class of legends called aetiological, *i.e.* invented to account for an existing custom or a name (p. 69). The goose was a bird sacred to Juno, and it acquired this honour not by the achievement of the watchful defenders of the Capitol, for the fact of geese being kept in the sanctuary of Juno at the time of the siege shows that the custom was older than that date. There was an annual festival in honour of Juno, celebrated with a public procession, in which geese were carried through the town on soft cushions and festively adorned, whilst dogs were nailed on boards. The story of the neglect of the dogs and the watchfulness of the geese was probably invented to account for this ancient custom. The share of Manlius in the saving of the Capitol may have been inferred from his name Capitolinus, a name derived more probably from his residence on the Capitoline hill.

<small>The story of the geese an aetiological legend.</small>

Whatever may have been the duration of the occupation of Rome by the Gauls, and however extensive the destruction caused by the invasion, it is certain that the injury done to the republic was not vital. On the contrary, the material losses seem to have been soon repaired. The city was rebuilt in a very short time; the ascendency of Rome over her dependent allies, if it was weakened momentarily, was soon fully re-established, and, what is more important than all this, the framework of the constitution bore the strain of disastrous war without giving way in any part. When the storm had passed over and the damage which it had caused was repaired, Rome continued her career of internal reform and foreign conquests, not merely with unimpaired but with invigorated energy. Only fourteen years after the battle of the Allia, Licinius and Sextius began the agitation for the equal division of the consular power between patricians and plebeians, which ten years later led to the Licinian laws (366 B.C.). In the year 387 B.C.—only three years after the Gallic catastrophe—the first great addition was made to the Roman territory. Four new tribes were formed out of the conquered Veientine land and added to the original twenty-one tribes to which the republic had been limited for 120 years. Twenty-nine years later (358 B.C.) two more tribes were added from acquisitions in Latium, and at the same time the league with the Latins was renewed on a fresh basis, which made Latium practically a dependency of Rome. A few years later (354 B.C.) the spreading influence and increasing power of Rome appears in the conclusion of a treaty of friendship with the great nation of the Samnites. In 348 B.C. a commercial treaty was concluded with Carthage, and in 343 B.C.—not half-a-century after the invasion of the Gauls—Rome was powerful enough to enter on that long-continued struggle with the Samnites which resulted in the acquisition of undoubted supremacy in Italy. It may well be doubted whether the Gauls had done more harm or more good to the Roman people by their invasion of Italy. If Rome was paralysed for a moment by the blow on the Allia, perhaps the neighbours of Rome were more vitally injured, and thus the relative strength of Rome increased. Besides, the Gauls were now looked upon as the natural enemies of all the native races of Italy, and as they continued their periodical invasions for a considerable time, Rome acquired by degrees the position of a defender of the common soil, and the right to unite the Italians into a large confederation. This confederation, under the Roman leadership, was the mighty state which in the succeeding generations overthrew Carthage, the kingdoms of Macedon and Syria, the commonwealths of Greece, the barbarians of northern Italy and Spain, and which when it had outgrown the forms of federal and republican institutions, was changed into an absolute military monarchy, which completed the work of conquest.

INDEX.

Administration of justice, 117
Aediles, 137
Aeneas, 30
Aequians, decay of, 183
Aequian wars, 148
Aetiological myths, 69
Agrarian laws, 144
Alba Longa, head of confederacy, 82
Allia, battle of, 196
Alliance of Romans and Sabines, 84
Amulius, 31
Ancus Martius, 43
Annalists, 14, 15, 28, 29
Antium, 153
Anxur, 185
Appius Claudius, 165
Ardea, 184
Aricia, 184
Assembly of centuries, 128
Association of gentes, 7
Asylum of Romulus, 33
Athens, embassy to, 163
Attus Navius, 46; the augur, 86
Augurs, 120
Auspices, 98; formality of, 120; used for political purposes, 120

Beaufort, 11
Bolae, 185
Brennus, 199
Brutus, 56, 58

Caere, 193
Camillus, 198; criticism of history of, 202; military reforms of, 188
Canuleian law, 171
Capena, 193

Capitol, defence of the, 198
Censorship, 176; of morals, 180; limited, 181
Centuriate assembly, 50
Chronicles, family, 27
Chronological impossibilities, 65
Cincinnatus, 153, 176
Cincius Alimentus, 14
Claudian family, 161
Clients, 111
Cloaca maxima, 47
Cloelia, 62
Clusium, siege of, 195
Comitia centuriata, 128; military character of, 128
Comitia curiata, origin of the, 129, 133; superseded, 127
Comitia tributa, 109, 141, 170
Consular office, 113; duties of, 117
Coriolanus, 149
Cornelius Cossus, 185
Cossus, Cornelius, 185
Credulity of the old historians, 10
Cremera, Roman fort on the, 156
Curiae, assembly of, 108
Curtian lake, 34, 70
Curtius, 34

Decemvirs, 162
Delphi, oracle of, consulted, 55
Delphian Apollo, 192
Descent of Roman people, 4
Dictator, 102
Dictatorship, 114; origin of, 115
Divination, 98
Duumviri perduellionis, 101

Epic poems wanting in Rome, 90

206   Index.

EPI

Epic poetry of Greece, 89
Etruscan dominion in Latium, 86
Etruscan war, 156
Etruscans, decline of, 194
Evidence, contemporary, 13; second-hand, 13
Extent of Roman empire, 1

Fabii, before Clusium, 195; disaster of the, 157
Fabius Pictor, 14
Falerii, 193
Family portraits, 26
Family, Roman, 24
Faustulus, 31
Fiction, 17
Fidenae, 155, 185
Financial duties of the censors, 181
Funerals, 26
Funeral orations, 26

Gabii, 54
Gauls, 187; migration of the, 194; destruction of Rome by the, 200
Geographical situation of Rome, 4, 6
Gibbon, 11

Hierarchical character of civil communities, 91
Horatii and Curiatii, 41
Horatius Cocles, 60
Hostus Hostilius, 34

Imperium, 114
Inauguration of the king, 101
Intercession, right of, 113, 135
Intermarriage between patricians and plebeians, 168, 171
Interreges, 101
Interregnum, 37, 106

Jupiter Capitolinus, temple of, 47
Jurisdiction, public and private, 117
Jus auxilii of tribunes, 137, 139

King of Sacrifices, rex sacrorum, lowered in authority, 118
King, sacerdotal, 100

PON

Labici, 185
Larentia, 31
Lars Tolumnius, 185
Latin war, 62, 80
Laudations, 27
Law, influence of Rome, 2
Laws of kings, 23
Laws, origin of, 68; of the twelve tables, 162
League with the Latins and Hernicans, 145
Legends of kings, 30
Lewis, Sir G. C., 12
Lex curiata, 114
Lex curiata de imperio, 109
Lex sacrata, 136
Lucretia, 56

Magister Populi, 102, 106, 115
Manlius, defence of the capitol, 199
Master of the horse, 114
Mettius Fufetius, 42
Military monarchy in Rome, 87; pay, 189; tribunes, 182; tribunes with consular power, 172
Mons sacer, 136
Montesquieu, 11
Monuments, public, 24
Mucius Scaevola, 61
Mythology, adoption of the Greek, 93

Nepete, 192
Niebuhr, 11
Numa and Ancus identified, 75
Numa Martius, 39
Numa Pompilius, 37
Numitor, 31

Oaths, 137
Ostia, 44

Patres, 105; conscripti, 124
Patricians, 108; influence of, on elections, 174; predominance of, 131
Patrum auctoritas, 106
Pecunia, 143
People in the regal period, 107
Plebeians, 108; rights of, 110
Plebeian senators, 122
Plebs, origin of, 110
Poems, historical, 16, 18
Pontiffs, 97, 103; interpreters of divine

and human law, 118; guardians of science and learning, 187
Pontifical annals, 21; burning of, 22
Pontius Cominius, 198
Poplicola, 115
Porcius Cato, 14
Porsenna, 60, 78
Porta Carmentalis, 158
Praeneste, 183
Praetor maximus, 102, 115
Praetors, 113
Priests, 97; kings of Rome, 85; public servants, 118
Public documents, 22
Public land, 143
Publilian law, 159

Quaestores Parricidii, 101
Quaestors elected by the people, 169; doubled in number, 181
Quirinus, 36

Rape of the Sabines, 33, 69
Rationalistic explanation of fables, 64
Relics, legendary, 23
Religion, age of, 68, 85; as a legal system, 96; meaning of the word, 95; of the Romans, 92, 94; purely national, 91
Religious institutions, great antiquity of, 90, 92
Rex sacrorum, 104
Rhea Silvia, 31
Roman armies, 188
Rome, a Latin settlement, 82; destruction of by the Gauls, 200
Romulus, legend of, 72
Romulus and Remus, legend of, 31
Romulus and Tarquinius identified, 75
Romulus and Tullus identified, 74

Sabines, invasion of, 83
Sacerdotal king superseded, 85

Sacred law, 137
Secession, causes of, 136; of the plebs, 135
Senate, a consultative body, 122; character and stability of, 126; of the regal period, 104; purely patrician, 124; not a representative assembly, 125
Senators, added by Brutus, 122; mode of electing, 126; number of, 122
Servian constitution, origin of, 77
Servilius Ahala, 176
Servius Tullius, 75
Sibylline books, 55
Spolia opima, 185
Spurius Cassius, 144, 147
Spurius Maelius, 175
Sutrium, 187, 192

Tanaquil, 44
Tarpeia, 33
Tarquinii, 193
Tarquinius Priscus, 45
Tarquinius, reforms of, 46
Tarquinius Superbus, 53
Tenure of land, 43
Terentilian rogations, 160
Titus Tatius, 35
Tradition, 14, 18, 29
Tribes, local, 140; old patrician, 35
Tribunes, antiquity of, 138; election of, 139; number of, 139; of the people, 135; sacrosancti, 136
Tribute or war tax, 140
Tullus Hostilius, 40

Valerian, laws, 116
Valerius, 115
Veii, 186; siege of, 190; capture of, 190
Vesta, 38
Vico, 11
Virginia, 166
Volscians, decay of, 183
Volscian Wars, 148

www.ingramcontent.com/pod-product-compliance
Lightning Source LLC
Chambersburg PA
CBHW021832230426
43669CB00008B/950